FORGOTTEN RAILWAYS:

North and Mid Wales

THE FORGOTTEN RAILWAYS SERIES

Edited by J. Allan Patmore

North East England by K. Hoole
The East Midlands by P. Howard Anderson
Chilterns and Cotswolds by R. Davies and M. D. Grant

Other volumes are in the course of preparation

BY THE SAME AUTHOR

The Cambrian Railways: Volumes 1 and 2
(with R. W. Miller)
The North Staffordshire Railway
(with R. W. Miller)
A Regional History of the Railways of Great Britain:
Volume 7—*The West Midlands*

FORGOTTEN RAILWAYS:

North and Mid Wales

REX CHRISTIANSEN

DAVID & CHARLES

NEWTON ABBOT LONDON

NORTH POMFRET (VT) VANCOUVER

ISBN 0 7153 7059 6
Library of Congress Catalog Card Number 75-31317

Set in 11 on 13 Baskerville
and printed in Great Britain
by Latimer Trend & Company Ltd Plymouth
for David & Charles (Holdings) Limited
Brunel House Newton Abbot Devon

Published in the United States of America
by David & Charles Inc
North Pomfret Vermont 05053 USA

Published in Canada
by Douglas David & Charles Limited
132 Philip Avenue North Vancouver BC

Contents

List of Illustrations

7

Maps, Diagrams and Drawings in Text

9

MAPS, DIAGRAMS AND DRAWINGS IN TEXT

CHAPTER 1

Lines Living and Unforgettable

Flavours and joys

Let my first words reassure. For while there are enough closed railways in North and Mid Wales comfortably to fill this book, enough standard and narrow gauge lines remain open to fill another. There is the splendid Chester & Holyhead, with the open deck of the rebuilt Britannia Bridge over the Menai Strait giving travellers the glorious panoramas of water and mountain of which they were robbed when trains used to plunge into the single-line tubes. (Reconstruction has made doubly precious my memory of riding through the smoke-filled tube on the footplate of Royal Scot 46127 *Old Contemptibles* hauling the Irish Mail.)

The lovely hill, river, and lake route between Ruabon and Barmouth may have gone, but part is being revived by the narrow gauge Bala Lake Railway, and there are still the delights to enjoy of the Cambrian main line to Aberystwyth and the coast line. There are other narrow gauge lines, including the Festiniog, soon to return to Blaenau Ffestiniog and provide a change-of-gauge route for tourists who also use that superb, much under-rated and neglected scenic feast through the Conway Valley. There is still, although used only by occasional passenger specials, the Conway line's new-found extension from Blaenau Ffestiniog to the nuclear power station at Trawsfynydd.

The Llandudno branch packs as much river, mountain and distant historic scenery (Conway Castle) into its three miles as many a line a dozen times longer. On Angelsey there is the 'breezy' Holyhead Breakwater Railway, running from a stone quarry on Holyhead Mountain for about two miles, mostly along the breakwater.

Bounding North Wales with its splendid viaducts and hilly route, is the Shrewsbury & Chester line (no longer a main one), from which stemmed busy and complicated railway systems at Ruabon and Wrexham. It still feeds the former GWR branch from Croes Newydd to Brymbo, and connects with the old Wrexham, Mold & Connah's Quay main line to Hawarden, on which two-coach diesel trains continue via Shotton to Birkenhead North, offering pleasant views on the journey through the Wirral Peninsula of the Dee estuary and its magnificent backcloth of the Welsh hills.

There was increasing pressure in 1974 for the opening of a new halt on this line at Aston, between Buckley and Shotton, to serve a new and growing commuter area, the idea no doubt being influenced by the successful reopening two years earlier of the Low Level platforms on the Chester & Holyhead at Shotton.

Not every station has been as lucky as Shotton, even though its new role is only that of an unstaffed halt. There are dozens of closed stations all over Wales that have since become houses or been incorporated into industrial premises (Buckley Junction is among them). In some places, as at Trevor, near Ruabon, stations have disappeared altogether or been vandalised (Dolgellau), or in exceptional cases survived virtually intact (Llangollen). The remaining ones are history's latest landmarks. While not as substantial or striking as the Welsh castles, the stations bear testimony to lost, though peaceful, economic battles, fought to prevent the ebb of railways from the countryside.

Unlike castles, stations are not unique symbols of past battles, for there are several other kinds of railway relics scattered about—tunnels and viaducts, signal boxes (occasionally signals), warehouses, and plentiful lengths of trackbed, generally overgrown, but sometimes used for country walks (Barmouth

Junction–Penmaenpool is among those most recently projected), or road improvements.

The disused lines of North and Mid Wales come in splendid variety, almost as different as the scenery itself. Lines of once similar character are to be found in contrasting settings. The LNWR secondary route from Bangor to the Cambrian coast at Afon Wen was much dominated by mountains with rugged outcrops; the same company's secondary route from Chester to Corwen, while also predominately rural, encircled the Clwydian Hills, which are anything but rugged. This route and its scenery was more akin to that of the GWR through the Dee Valley from Ruabon to Dolgellau.

Purely rural branches abounded. Webb tanks shedded at Bangor for many years worked to Red Wharf Bay in a flattish corner of Anglesey, a line used only for goods after 1930, while their shed mates pounded uphill to reach Bethesda with passenger trains and some goods.

Some branches were purely mineral lines for decades, like the Kerry, and its neighbour at some distance, the Van Railway. Some lines were purely private and ephemeral—the Elan Valley Railway, near Rhayader, fulfilled that concept.

To those with only a generalised knowledge of North Wales, the idea that it was purely rural was easily destroyed by the industry around Wrexham and Brymbo, where the GWR did not have all its own way. Architectural and railway spice was provided by the little Wrexham Mold & Connah's Quay. It was swallowed by the Great Central and after Grouping digested by the LNER, even though many people found it hard to stomach the idea of King's Cross (or strictly Marylebone, for that was the LNER headquarters) being represented in Wales. It took in the Buckley Railway, which tumbled downhill on almost alarming gradients to the little port of Connah's Quay. Mind you, there was never a danger of engines crashing through the buffers into the Dee, for guarding the docks approach was the smallest bridge imaginable under which only 'Hornby'-sized locomotives could ever squeeze. There were branches to other small ports such as Aberdovey on the Cambrian, while Port Penrhyn and Port Dinorwic developed to export Snowdonian slate by sea. These two latter ports were strongholds of the Penrhyn and Padarn narrow gauge systems.

Narrow gauge lines find no place in this book. This perhaps startling admission can be easily justified. The narrow gauge companies, dead or revived, have been extensively chronicled and the main purpose of this book is to evoke the memory of standard gauge railways which, by and large, were never so well-known because their existence was taken for granted.

Standard gauge revivals have taken place everywhere in Britain except North Wales, but that may be rectified soon through the enthusiasm of the Cambrian Railways Society at Oswestry, which has bought a Manor class 4-6-0 (one which worked mainly on the Cambrian section) and hopes to get steam working again between Gobowen and Nantmawr on the BR retained quarry line. Another group actively pursuing a steam revival is the Flint & Deeside Preservation Society, which at the time of writing, was hoping to reopen a short section between Ruabon–Dolgellau.

Geographically, Oswestry is in England, not Wales, but this book includes the Oswestry, Ellesmere & Whitchurch because it ran through the detached part of the former County of Flint, now Clwyd. Not all Mid Wales lines are included in this collection: only the Mid Wales Railway between Moat Lane and Brecon—other routes to Brecon, and lines south of Aberystwyth are ignored because a boundary has to be drawn somewhere. So it otherwise sweeps along the Cambrian line to Aberystwyth and northwards round the coast of North Wales back to Shotton.

What is to be got out of searching for old lines, especially in a region where the delights of the narrow gauge revived lure the heart? Better, I think, to consider the question another way. By travelling narrow gauge and searching for forgotten railways you can have two tickets for the price of one. A lost railways hunt can be a new family objective in the countryside and introduce them to remote places and to scenery which they might not otherwise have found to enjoy.

Scenery, however attractive, fades from the mind unless it is retained by personal association. I have known North Wales nearly all my life. My first holiday was at Colwyn Bay when at the age of 18 months I stayed beside the main line and spent, I'm told, most of the time watching trains. Nothing, it seems, delighted me more than those which raced through the station platforms where steam-hauled expresses reached symphonic climax as their roar reverberated around that glass-screened 'Hollywood Bowl' of a station.

However, I never came to know the North Wales scenery as intimately as I do now until beginning research for this book. Its mountains, hills, valleys and rivers are better identified in my mind by lost railways. Unlike scenery, railway detail needs to be stored in places other than the mind. That is one reason why this book is divided, in a sense, into two. The chapters seek to evoke the railways that have gone, their setting and their services, but they are deliberately shorn of a multitude of exact and exacting details. Instead, far more than an appendix, is the other part of the book, the Gazetteer, a detailed guide, line by line, to places and remains.

Although the text supplements it, each section of the Gazetteer is self contained, being introduced by a short mood creating scene-set. Spellings that keep changing—Caernarvon is perhaps the best-known example—have caused problems. I have chosen to use a mixture of old and new spellings for the book deals with yesterday and today. The original spellings are those used by the old railway companies. The Gazetteer includes an outline history of each line and the location of remains that are worth visiting. It makes no claim to be exhaustive, if only because the uses to which old railway land and property are being put are changing constantly.

Occasionally these adaptations are in sympathy with the spirit of railways of old. At Dinas Mawddwy you will find two splendid gates guarding the entrance to a station that is a tearoom and a yard that houses a thriving woollen mill. Welsh craftsmen have restored the gates, which the little Mawddwy Railway once thought more important to provide than shelter for passengers at intermediate stops. Part of the trackbed has been adapted for a short narrow gauge line.

Near Wrexham, an old colliery line, which stemmed from the Wrexham Mold & Connah's Quay, is being adapted as a country park. A local amenity society helped by volunteers started work in September 1974 on a stretch more than a mile long between Caergwrle station and the New Inn at Cefnybedd.

Agitation continues from time to time for the re-opening of closed lines. The 1974 reprieve of the Cambrian Coast line prompted a suggestion for the restoration of the Bangor–Caernarvon–Afon Wen route, that was once complementary to it. The National Council on Inland Transport and the North Wales Railway Circle wrote to Gwynedd County Council, who were advised by the BR divisional manager at Stoke-on-Trent, Mr Frank Young. He said that relaying the track and restoring structures and signalling and providing rolling stock would cost £600,000. The County Council would have to underwrite the costs and Mr Young stated that on the basis of past experience it was doubtful if revenue would cover running costs. The Council considered the letter just before deciding to buy $6\frac{1}{2}$ miles of the trackbed northwards from Caernarvon, mainly for road improvements.

Page 17 (Above) The Kerry branch of the Cambrian, opened in 1863 was a financial embarrassment from the start, yet it managed to survive for passengers until 1931 and freight to 1956. The branch mixed train is seen here in the last century with 0–4–0ST No 36 *Plasfynnon* built for the line by Sharp, Stewart.

(Below) Llangollen: hill dominated station, still virtually intact apart from track, has been reopened by preservationists. The scene about 1909 with Ruabon bound train headed by 2–4–0 of the 3201 class, shedded at Croes Newydd, Wrexham, which regularly worked to Dolgelley.

Page 18 (Above) Wrexham Central station about 1900 with a Cambrian train to Ellesmere on right. Central remains terminus of dmus from Birkenhead North.

(Below) Ffrith Viaduct, LNWR/GWR Joint Line (Wrexham & Minera Extension Railway). The viaduct, photographed looking towards Brymbo in 1959, still survived as this book was in preparation.

CHAPTER 2

Wrexham

Chocolate & cream and apple green

Wrexham must be one of the few towns of modest size that can still be approached by rail from three directions—Chester, Birkenhead (via the Wrexham, Mold & Connah's Quay) and Shrewsbury. They remain the main routes of an area that once had so many lines belonging to competing companies that Railway Clearing House maps of Lancashire & District needed enlarged sections to show them all.

Within five miles of the town lay the most complex area in North Wales for collieries, steelworks and quarries, knitted together by railways. The Denbighshire Coalfield on which the fortunes of Wrexham and Ruabon, its neighbour to the south, depended totally in the last century, has now been reduced to a single pit: Bersham, beside the Shrewsbury & Chester main line.

Wrexham, by far the largest town in Wales north of the valleys of South Wales, was an early focus of the industrial revolution and industry was well established long before railways were built. After grouping, trains of two of the Big Four—GWR and LNER—were prominent, while those of the LMS reached the fringes of the area.

There were two focal points of the system; Wrexham, and nearly four miles away in the hills, Brymbo, where a large steelworks was developed. Today it makes specialised steels and its prosperity has been responsible for the retention of the ex-GWR branch. The works has a link with a forgotten railway in Oxfordshire for the Company had an iron ore mine close to the now closed branch between Banbury and Kingham, and its own

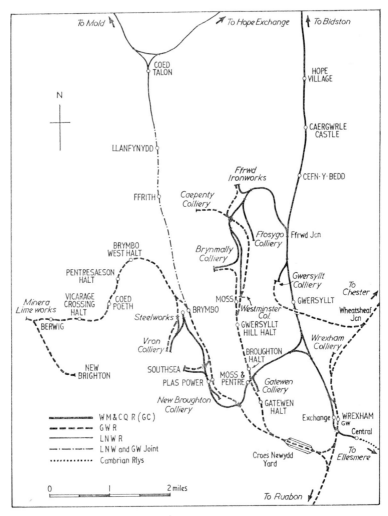

Wrexham, where competing lines, big and small, filled local valleys

siding near Hook Norton, from where trains carried ore to Brymbo. The Brymbo branch leaves the S & C main line at Croes Newydd and runs up a steepening, narrowing valley to the works, which have been extended on a man-made cliff and which dominate the village.

A periodic depression in the iron and steel trades delayed the arrival of the railway at Wrexham. The first was planned in 1839 by businessmen to run from Chester, twelve miles away. They commissioned George Stephenson while the Crewe and Chester and Chester and Birkenhead lines were under construction. Five years elapsed without anything being done, and it was not until 1844 that positive moves were made with the formation of the North Wales Mineral Railway. At that time coal from North Wales was having to be taken nearly sixty miles by canal to reach Chester, being dispatched from Pontcysyllte wharf near the famous aqueduct, in barges that voyaged via Ellesmere, Whitchurch and Nantwich.

Railways were ideal for the Wrexham area because they were the most efficient means of handling the major commodities produced, or used by industry: coal, limestone and steel. An attempt to build the Ellesmere Canal in a direct line between the Dee at Chester and the Severn at Shrewsbury failed in the difficult terrain around Wrexham. The North Wales Mineral Railway put Wrexham on the railway map in 1846 and other lines quickly followed, although the early ones were rather unsatisfactory.

Brymbo & Minera Branch

Most guide books ignore Brymbo, yet this area, so much ravaged by industry and its needs, is full of scenic surprises. You feel its character the moment you begin exploring the branch of the North Wales Mineral Railway, which struck into the hills from Wheatsheaf Junction, just north of Wrexham. It followed an almost impossible course through the intervening ridges or over them. Two tunnels and two rope-worked inclines were needed within a short distance. The inclines were called brakes—a tag commemorated by the Brake Methodist Church at Moss opened in 1885. It stands at the top of what used to be the second incline, close to the second tunnel mouth.

Much of the line has been obliterated by housing and landscaping in recent years, but sufficient remains to make a survey rewarding. A good impression of the sort of country that the builders had to tackle can be gained by standing on the Wrexham–Mold road (A541) at Gwersyllt where beside the Wheatsheaf Inn there is an abutment of a track underbridge that led to the first incline. The use of inclines enabled the line to be built almost arrow straight for much of the way and its progress uphill from the Wheatsheaf Inn can be traced by going on to a housing estate built a little farther up the hill. Two sections of the estate are divided by a pathway overhung by trees planted on what was obviously a low embankment of the incline. It is worth seeing. Inclines were not novel by the time the line was opened in 1847, well over a year ahead of the completion of the Shrewsbury & Chester (as the NWMR had become) south from Ruabon to Shrewsbury.

With the closing of Gresford Colliery in October 1973, the Wrexham area was left with only Bersham pit. But more than a century before, dozens of pits had been sunk into rich seams and they were working long before the railways arrived. Despite its steep inclines, the Brymbo branch was a most successful spearhead into an area where transport was needed for coal, limestone and iron products. One incline was still in use after 1862 when the present branch from Croes Newydd was taken up a neighbouring valley on gradients which, while they remained stiff, were workable without cable assistance.

The GWR initiative did not spell the end of the original Brymbo & Minera branch, and the short line had the distinction of being closed in four sections. The route from Wheatsheaf Junction through Summerhill Tunnel into the Moss Valley was in use until October 1908, when it was cut back to Gwersyllt, where a spur continued to serve local pits. Paddington faced competition here from the WM & CQ. The Brymbo branch served a brickworks until it was cut back to Wheatsheaf Junction about 1951. That left the most westerly section between the GWR branch at Brymbo and limestone quarries at Minera. The end of rail-borne quarry traffic in 1972 removed one of the Stoke-on-Trent Division's most complicated operating hazards—

eight gated and unmanned crossings on a short line. Traces of all remain

Until the opening of the branch from Croes Newydd and the improvement of the GWR Moss Valley branch twenty years later, Brymbo traffic was marshalled in a large yard at Wheat-

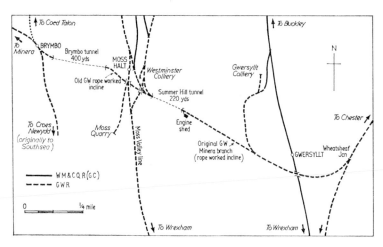

The North Wales Mineral Railway—in the region, the only major standard gauge line with inclines

sheaf. Even after a number of sidings were lifted during World War I, the yard remained busy and had a capacity for 269 wagons. But by 1924 it had fallen into disfavour, a Chester Division report stating:

> The Yard is in a very exposed position and only Colliery empties are put there occasionally for stabling purposes.

The GWR and WM & CQ (and its successor the Great Central) fought for traffic at Vron, another exposed part of the area, high in the hills about a mile from Brymbo. The GWR was first there with a branch of no more than $1\frac{1}{4}$ miles from Brymbo Middle Signalbox. It was authorised in 1845 and opened about the time of the original Brymbo branch two years later. The

WM & CQ also thought it worthwhile to serve Vron Colliery, constructing a ¾-mile dog-leg which was opened in 1888, soon after the completion of its branch to Brymbo and a single-platform passenger station much farther down the hillside than that of the GWR.

The branch was authorised in 1882 and opened after five years had been spent cutting through the countryside from a junction with the WM & CQ main line north of Wrexham (quite close to Wheatsheaf Junction) and sweeping across rising ground west of Wrexham to reach the same valley as Paddington chose for its second branch. The routes crossed at Plas Power, the locally-inspired line following the opposite side of the valley from its rival. At Grouping it became the most westerly branch of the LNER, which continued to work daily trains to Vron Colliery long after the GWR had ceased to do so because it was considered that by 1924 'the output does not warrant a service'. The pit closed in 1930, but parts of the Vron branch can still be traced.

The WM & CQ station was buried when the man-made hillside at Brymbo was extended for the steelworks. The GWR Vron branch survives, although it was shortened after the pit closure. It still gives access to the steelworks, and in 1973 sidings near the Colliery site were enlarged to handle extra traffic. From the branch, a back shunt runs inside the works to the blast furnaces. It is used by the company's diesels, not BR trains, but they still pass through the centre of the works, being shunted from Brymbo West to a small group of sidings.

The WM & CQ route to Brymbo was more than a mile longer than Paddington's. Wrexham Central was central while the General station was about half a mile from the shops. But at Brymbo, the WM & CQ locals finished up at a terminus at the bottom of a valley while most of the local houses were grouped above. The GWR locals stopped half way up that hill.

This was one of the few branches on which the Great Central ran steam railmotors, but they did not provide the traffic hoped for and the service was withdrawn in 1917. Paddington persevered with its locals, which ran through to Berwig, until 1931.

24

British Rail did better, retaining the LMS Mold link until 1950. The WM & CQ branch closed for good in 1970, but not before several modifications. In 1954 a new connection was put in with the GWR branch at Plas Power and the link to Brymbo Works was re-opened to goods. It closed in 1958, only to enjoy a revival between 1965–70. The connection had allowed the lifting of the section from Plas Power to Brymbo Junction of the WM & CQ. It included what had been a quarter-mile spur from the line to Gatewen Colliery in the Moss Valley, which the GWR had also served.

Moss Valley Branches

Inclines were needed to take the original Brymbo branch in and out of the Moss Valley, which lay between Wheatsheaf Junction and the steel town. But the Moss Valley was also rich in coal and heavily industrialised by the time railways arrived. Ffrwd Iron-works and Colliery in the upper end of the valley had opened sometime before 1796. Westminster Colliery opened in primitive form some years earlier, was improved in 1846 and extended once the Brymbo inclines opened, and its coal could be trans-ported easily out of the valley. Another local pit, Brynmally, was among the oldest in the district and its owners sunk others in-cluding Ffrosygo. It was to serve these that the Shrewsbury & Chester was authorised to build a branch from Wheatsheaf to Minera in 1846. This new line opened the following year, and the GWR (with which the S & C had merged in 1854) en-joyed a monopoly of the valley's coal output until the WM & CQ opened its Ffrwd branch. This was included in its Act of Incorporation in 1862 and opened at the same time as the main line to Buckley four years later. The branch was profitable and was used until the last pit, Brynmally, closed in 1935. The first half mile survived as a shunting neck to sidings alongside the WM & CQ main line.

Competition—and the growth of local villages—encouraged the GWR to build the Moss Valley branch, sanctioned by Parliament in 1882. It ran two miles from Croes Newydd yard

25

up the valley to Moss, where it joined the original North Wales Mineral Railway branch (via the lower of the two original Brymbo Inclines) to Brynmally Colliery, half a mile beyond Moss. The colliery branch followed the west side of the Moss Valley, the NWMR Ffrwd branch was built on the opposite side.

Paddington introduced a local passenger service into the valley, something that its rival, the WM & CQ, never attempted. Railmotors were considered adequate for traffic needs and from 1905 to 1930 they called at halts at Gatewen (close to Moss & Pentre halt on the WM & CQ Brymbo branch, which passed under the Moss line); Pentre Broughton, Gwersyllt, and Moss, a railhead, claimed Paddington, for 14,000 people living in three villages. For years there was talk of withdrawing the railmotors, but they were retained until overwhelming competition came from buses, which could run quicker and more directly to shopping and other amenities at Wrexham.

Administratively, the Moss Valley branch was forgotten from its closure in 1935, but physically it lingered, the track remaining in position until 1952. Some of it is back again, for the coal industry has taken on a new lease of life with the exploitation of extensive opencast workings in the hills near Vron, quite close to Brymbo steelworks.

A railhead for the coal was developed on the site of Gatewen Colliery and served at first from the stub of the WM & CQ Brymbo branch, part of which was relaid. More recently, about a mile of the GWR branch has been put back from near Moss Valley Junction by a contractor, and two sidings laid at Gatewen. Wagons are loaded by conveyor from coal bunkers fed by lorry. A shunting neck extends about 50yd north of the bridge that used to carry the line over the Brymbo branch. A section of this old line has been converted into a road and lorries run under the Moss line to reach the bunkers. The contractor uses either his own diesel shunter, or one hired from BR.

Wrexham & Minera Extension Joint Railway

Anyone rummaging among waste land that lies within the shadow of the steelworks will come across the crumbling remains of the edges of the long-demolished Brymbo GWR station. Heading away from the line at the Minera end he may notice a trackbed, which runs under an iron-framed road bridge of venerable age. Such was the exit from Brymbo of one of those railways which never went near where its title stated. The Wrexham & Minera Extension Joint Railway ran northwards towards the little village of Coed Talon. On weekday mornings until 1950, a small tank engine would arrive at Brymbo, collect two coaches from a siding that lay amid what is now long grass at what was the Wrexham end of the station. Then it would chuff off towards Mold, the fireman no doubt happy to take advantage of the gradient falling away from the station to relax a little from his labours. The line, besides being joint, had an interesting history but that is described in Chapter 8 because it had generally closer affinities with lines around Mold rather than the Wrexham complex.

The Buckley Railway

The Joint Line gave the LNWR its closest track to Wrexham, hardly satisfactory, yet its influence would have been far stronger in the area had it taken up an option to contribute a third of the £30,000 initial capital of the Buckley Railway, formed in 1860. The private company took its title from a town twelve miles north of Wrexham, which was the thriving hub of coal mines, brickworks and clay quarries. Their owners launched the railway to get their products to the sea, using the small tidal port of Connah's Quay five miles away on the Dee estuary, where a junction was also established with the Chester & Holyhead line.

Any attempt to survey the remains of the Buckley Railway will take one 'round the houses', for parts of the trackbed have

27

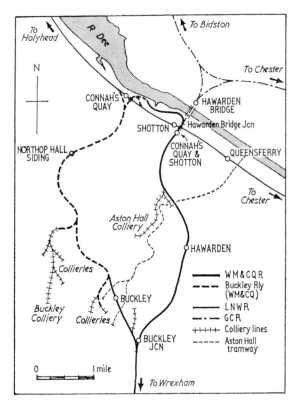

Buckley mines and brickworks were served progressively by tramways, a railway local in concept, and the wider-ranging WM & CQR

been over-built by new estates. Little of the line remains, but there is sufficient to rekindle the flames of memory. The most evocative bits are at Connah's Quay, where the derelict station which the Buckley shared with the main line retains a certain dignity, which vandals have failed to strip. There is a mass of undergrowth where sidings once lay—a pleasant, wooded thicket. The Buckley was a fascinating company that had five owners in 105 years, becoming one of the Welsh outposts of the Great Central and the LNER.

Besides being single, the Buckley route was one of cruel

gradients; it fell for two miles at between 1 in 30 and 1 in 48. Embankments, built wherever possible, did little to relieve the lie of the line. To the end it was rather primitive, being without passing loops. It was reputed to have been constructed partly over an old tramway from Northop Hall (Dublin Main Colliery) to Connah's Quay. Two months after its opening (7 June 1862), its destiny was foreshadowed, despite the annoyance of itself and Paddington, by the birth of the WM & CQ.

The Buckley Railway's individuality effectively vanished after a working agreement signed when the line opened, and strengthened by a 999-year lease to that company from 1873. It lasted far short of even 99 years, for both companies were swallowed into the Great Central in 1905. It was not unexpected, for the Manchester, Sheffield & Lincolnshire had driven successfully from North-east Cheshire to Chester and bridged the Dee at Hawarden Bridge, just short of Connah's Quay, where the river broadens into a wide estuary. The Cheshire line was driven towards Wrexham by the $4\frac{1}{2}$-mile Hawarden Loop of 1890. In essence, it duplicated the Buckley Railway, about a mile to the north, but the Loop gradients were a little less severe, 1 in 53 at worst.

Yet the Buckley Railway, for all its imperfections, continued to thrive. It was an adequate system for the traffic. A new station on the Hawarden Loop was built to serve Buckley. It was called Buckley Junction, a misnomer, since passenger trains never ran on the Buckley Railway. The Junction station was too remote from local industry, and local trains continued to shuttle over the WM & CQ branch to Buckley (the northern terminus of the main line) and to Buckley Old Station, as the original one was renamed.

If a new station were opened as has been suggested, to serve Aston, on the outskirts of Queensferry it would be in keeping with trends on Deeside, where industrial patterns are changing.

In recent years the small, yet once vigorous, docks at Connah's Quay have been transformed into an industrial estate. Alongside, the quays lie rotting, and on a misty morning when the

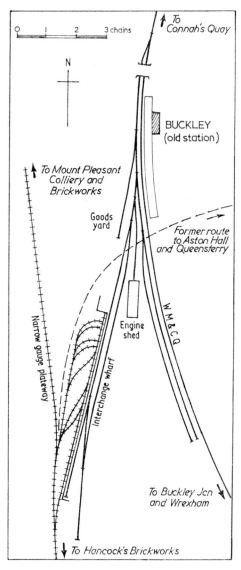

Buckley in detail—small, busy and varied

deep brown river eddies around them, it is a sad place. Yet the docks are a place to go if you want something to muse upon that is a little different. Their value was once real enough to the author of *Flintshire's Industrial Handbook*, published shortly before nationalisation.

> The importance of Connah's Quay is increased by the fact that the L&NER own the wharves, which are well equipped for the rapid handling of traffic, the equipment being two steam cranes of five tons, two of about three tons; several hand cranes and two excellent grabs have been recently added. Furthermore, the Company have recently spent some £7,000 in improving the wharves and connection is made at Connah's Quay with the LMSR system.

This was achieved by a line of just over a mile opened at the same time as the Hawarden Loop (31 May 1890). It ran from Shotton to Connah's Quay docks and gave the Great Central a connection with the Buckley Railway. A footpath, heavily flanked by scrub, runs along the low embankment of the line, parallel, on the river side, to the Chester & Holyhead. The path is within sight of Shotton Low Level station on the Chester & Holyhead, which became nationally prominent on 17 August 1972 when it was *re-opened*.

Shotton steelworks have helped to keep alive passenger traffic on the WM & CQ between Wrexham and Birkenhead North. For years operating losses have been made by two-coach dmus, which compensate in nippy performance for what they lack in looks compared with LNER class C13 Atlantic tanks, which maintained passenger services for years, from 1905, including the whole of World War II. There are hopes that it may be developed as a roundabout route between Chester and Wrexham to allow the closure of the Shrewsbury & Chester route, sorely troubled by subsidence on Gresford Bank. Developing the WM & CQ would involve the re-opening to passengers of the line between Chester and Shotton.

31

Horse and Castle!

While the Castles, Manors and Halls joined with Moguls and
2-8-0s to pound the Shrewsbury & Chester main line, Wrexham's branches and secondary lines were tank-glorious, burning
out their hearts on heavy coal trains on heavy gradients, or
more gently pulling passenger trains of up to half a dozen, but
generally no more than four, coaches. Passenger traffic never
demanded more. Ancient towns like Mold and hill-dominated
villages like Caergwrle (Castle & Wells, was the full title of the
station at one time), were self-contained communities, where
homes and industry lay close together.

In early days, every variety of traction was used. The Buckley
Railway was worked for years by horses. They might have enjoyed plodding slowly down the Flintshire slopes to the river,
but hardly the return journey, uphill all the way. The original
Brymbo branch never carried regular passenger services but
on the opening of the North Wales Mineral Railway between
Chester and Ruabon in 1847, the same year as the branch, an
excursion was run to Birkenhead. It is not known if the passengers were lowered down the inclines, but it seems unlikely.

Reminiscences handed through generations by word of mouth
rather than record, suggest that there were occasional excursions,
too, on the Buckley Railway. More worthy of memory are the
operating difficulties that the company suffered through that
impossibly low bridge under the Coast road. Goods trains from
Buckley always stopped short of the bridge, the locomotives
running round to propel wagons to be picked up by a shunter
which reached the dock over the spur from Shotton High Level.
In LNER days, some 0-6-0Ts of class J72 were given small
chimneys, but they still could not get under the bridge: there
was never a suggestion to rebuild it.

The WM & CQ main line in late Victorian years was carrying
a heavy service and the company was running ten trains each
way to Brymbo on Saturdays; and a more modest four on week-

days—equal to the GWR service. There were never Sunday trains on local lines.

Great Western branches were worked by locomotives stationed at Croes Newydd, o–4–2 tanks usually handling passenger trains and o–6–o pannier tanks the freight. Class 5600 o–6–2 tanks were used as far as Brymbo.

Operating was conventional; in later years, one engine in steam with electric staff on the busier sections of single branches, and wooden ones on more remote sections. Elaborate safety precautions were taken at village level crossings: at Coed Poeth, station signals were slotted from a crossing ground frame. In the gatewoman's cottage (pay: 8s od a week plus 3s 6d bonus in 1924), there were block indicators, bells and telephones.

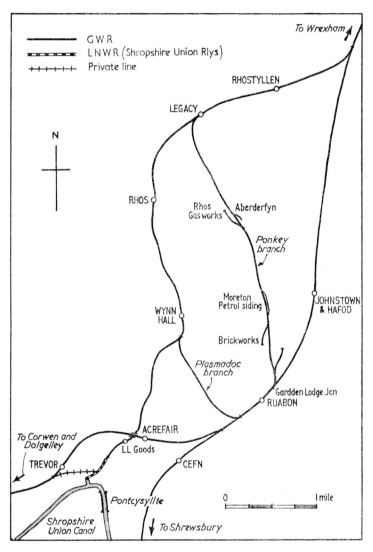

GWR
L N W R (Shropshire Union Rlys)
Private line

To Wrexham

RHOSTYLLEN

LEGACY

N

RHOS

Rhos Gasworks   Aberderfyn

Ponkey branch

Moreton Petrol siding

JOHNSTOWN & HAFOD

WYNN HALL

Brickworks

Plasmadoc branch

Gardden Lodge Jcn
RUABON

ACREFAIR

To Corwen and Dolgelley

LL Goods

TREVOR

CEFN

0   1 mile

Pontcysyllte

Shropshire Union Canal

To Shrewsbury

Ruabon—a busy, but little-known network

Page 35 (Above) Denbigh locomotive shed in 1952, where locomotives in semi-retirement often delighted the enthusiast. The shed still stands in an industrial estate.

(Below) A Great Western wayside halt – Legacy, south of Wrexham. Note the 'pagoda' lamp room, and generally ornate architecture.

Page 36 (Above) Berwyn, where the station building was tall and impressive, but passengers few. Ex-GWR pannier tank No 3789 begins to cross a short curved viaduct over a minor road, in 1963.

(Below) Corwen, junction for the Vale of Clwyd, in 1963. The station had two refreshment rooms among its facilities. Class 2 2–6–0 No 46509 stands with mineral empties at the down platform.

CHAPTER 3

GWR Branches

Ruabon: terra cotta and coal

Sixty-two men were employed at Ruabon at Grouping. It was a busy junction for Corwen, Dolgelley, the Cambrian Coast and Blaenau Ffestiniog. Controlled by five signal boxes, the Ruabon layout had thirty sidings for 700 wagons, small stables, 1st and 3rd class waiting rooms for ladies and gentlemen and two refreshment rooms. It was the hub of several branches to mines that made Ruabon brick and coal renowned throughout the country, and also to iron foundries, chemical works and quarries.

To go in search of Ruabon's lost railways is to go in search of forgotten industry, for while it is still an industrial area, it is nothing like it was at the turn of this century when the travel writer, A. G. Bradley, saw from afar its chimneys belching fire and smoke over the pastoral Dee Valley, just south of the town, at Pontcysyllte, and tagged the area as a 'horrid eyesore of modern growth'.

Belching chimneys have been replaced by the belching exhausts of vehicles on the busy road between Wrexham and the A5. Ruabon is no longer a junction and few passengers use its station, which from 1 April 1974 was reduced (with Chirk) to an unstaffed halt, and the station buildings were advertised to let.

Ponkey Branch

Branches around Ruabon were not as spectacular as those near Wrexham, but how the GWR thrived on them! The Ponkey

GREAT WESTERN RAILWAY.

(CHESTER DIVISION).

(For the use of the Company's Servants only).

SIGNAL DEPARTMENT WORK,
RUABON SOUTH.

The Signal Department will have occupation at Ruabon South from 7-0 a.m. **Sunday, October 19th,** to 5-0 p.m. on **Friday, October 24th,** or until the work is completed, for the purpose of bringing into use the following new Signals :—

Form	Name.	Position.	Distance from Box.
A	1. Up Main Starting for Middle Box 2. Up Inner Distant	Up side of Main Line	296 yards
B	1. Down Main Inner Home 2. Down Distant for Ruabon Middle 3. Down Main to Goods Running Loop. Inner Home	Down side of Line	8 yards
C	1. Down Main Home (Slotted from Llangollen Line Junction) 2. Down Main to Goods Running Loop Home	Down side of Line	239 yards

Discs will be fixed at the Points leading from Sidings, and at the Points of Crossover Road.

Not quite a forgotten railway: the Shrewsbury & Chester at Ruabon. Major re-signalling through the station in 1924 involved Llangollen Line Junction signal box branch which left the Shrewsbury & Chester line at Gardden Lodge on the goods loop just north of Ruabon station, ran for a little over a mile. Yet in that short distance it handled the traffic (economically operated by wooden staff and one engine in steam) of two brickworks, each with 40-wagon sidings, a petroleum company siding, and those of a furniture factory and the Rhos Gas Company which, incidentally, supplied Ruabon station for many years. All this happened on a branch that had actually been shortened as an economy! Until January 1917 it had run about half a mile beyond the village of Aberderfyn to Legacy. The section was soon lifted, but later a short siding (for twelve wagons) was laid at the Legacy end to provide access from the Rhos branch to a sub-station of the North Wales Power Company. After Grouping the GWR felt that 'there is no case for restoring' the closed section.

Those admiring the Pontcysyllte aqueduct and marvelling at the achievements of its builders in both crossing the Dee Valley and creating a structure of grace and beauty that enhanced the landscape, may not wish to have their thoughts of awe disturbed. But it was *railways* and not canals that brought Ruabon its industrial prosperity in late Victorian years. The canal promoters had planned to develop through the industrial hearts of Ruabon and Wrexham to reach the Dee at Chester. The remains at Ffrwd (page 25) are a monument to that venture, defeated by difficulties of finance, water and terrain. Yet the canal promoters can claim to have assisted the development of a tramway that was to blossom into a busy, profitable mineral railway—and then, in recent years, to die.

The tramway had a pretty name: Ruabon Brook. It was constructed by the Ellesmere Canal Company as a feeder from the canal at Pontcysyllte past the Plas Kynaston Ironworks & Colliery (the site of today's Monsanto Chemical Works), and Cefn stone quarries, to Acrefair village. In the primitive form of a double-track plateway, it was opened on 26 November 1805, and was extended three years later to a local pit, Plas Madoc. Subsequently its rails stretched to Wynn Hall Colliery, a mile south of Rhos. A branch crossed the S & C line to embrace Cefn Colliery.

Conversion of the tramway into a fully-fledged railway began in 1861 and involved a slightly deviated route. Parliament was not consulted, land being bought privately. Work began at Pontcysyllte and continued north in stages, the final one from Wynn Hall Colliery to Llwynenion Brickworks, just north of where Rhos station was later built. From opening in 1867, the railway was worked not by its owners, but by the New British Iron Company, which owned Wynnstay Colliery, and was a major source of traffic until it closed in 1886.

There were other changes: the Ellesmere Canal became part of the Shropshire Union Railways & Canal Company and from that concern, with Euston's consent, the GWR bought the line (Agreement 12 February 1896) for £51,000. The sale excluded lines at Pontcysyllte canal basin, which remained LNWR property.

Pontcysyllte canal-rail interchange traffic stopped before Grouping but the engine working between Pontcysyllte and Rhos continued to visit the basin for water.

A small GWR boiler for pumping water into the tank has been fixed in the old warehouse which at one time served as a transfer warehouse and also as an engine shed for the Shropshire Union Canal Company. A man is sent from Wrexham about twice a week to maintain the supply.

The man from Wrexham no longer goes to the basin (where the warehouse has been demolished), but pleasure boaters come ashore at the basin in their hundreds. Apart from the S & C, railways have left the area, though the canal flourishes again in the new era of leisure use. Since closure, the leisure use of the trackbed at Pant has caused problems. Cyclists, using it as a short cut, caused traffic hazards when they rode non-stop out on to a local road. The Council erected bollards to restrict the use of the trackbed to pedestrians.

Rails to Rhos

Railways never stamped their personality on the area south of Wrexham as they did in the hills around Brymbo. While the Brymbo lines were easy to find, the short 3¼-mile branch to Rhos hid itself among flattish fields and generally got lost among them. It was one of the means by which Paddington welded the Pontcysyllte—Rhos line on to its master system. It left the S & C at Rhos Junction, about a mile south of Wrexham General and ran towards Rhostyllen (where a station was built) and Legacy, which received a halt, controlled by the station-master at Rhos, a mile farther down the line.

The line developed into a busy outlet, mainly for two large brickworks, and Rhos was a busy little station, staffed by a dozen men, including two signalmen who worked at Legacy. Rhos had a small goods yard (capacity, with loops, 87 wagons), but no facilities for horses and cattle, although occasionally they were dealt with at the passenger station. Normally livestock handling was Legacy's role.

By the 1920s, Rhos was a small but busy mining community of about 12,000 people, and Paddington made several efforts to operate worthwhile passenger services before conceding defeat to local buses and the busy Wrexham–Rhos electric street tramway. Passenger trains were introduced between Wrexham and Rhos in 1901, and four years later extended just over 1½ miles to near Wynn Hall Colliery. That section survived until World War I, when the Ponkey branch was partly closed; the Wrexham–Rhos passenger service ceased in 1930, though Saturday soccer specials continued for Wrexham home games for some two decades.

Complementary to the northern extension through Rhos, the Pontcysyllte line was extended at the south end to Trevor goods yard on the Ruabon–Llangollen line. A quarter-mile section between the station and Trefynant brickworks had been constructed by the owners, J. C. Edwards. The GWR worked over

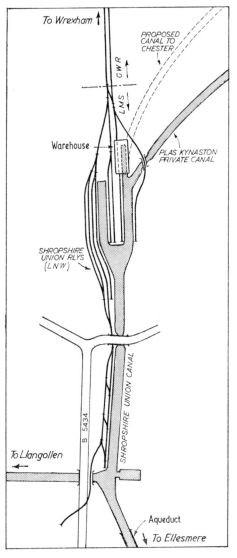

To Wrexham

PROPOSED CANAL TO CHESTER

GWR

LMS

Warehouse

PLAS KYNASTON PRIVATE CANAL

SHROPSHIRE UNION RLYS (LNW)

B 5434

SHROPSHIRE UNION CANAL

To Llangollen

Aqueduct

To Ellesmere

Pontcysyllte—a few yards of track gave the LNWR and the LMS their shortest and remotest outpost by agreement and it was used only for goods. Railtours were never allowed to use the section, specials having to reverse towards Wrexham.

Plas Madoc Branch

Pontcysyllte canal basin remained very much an isolated LNWR possession because the 1896 sale also included a short mineral line called the Plas Madoc branch. It ran from the down sidings half a mile south of Ruabon station, the junction being put in underneath a bridge carrying a private line to Wynnstay Colliery. Trains ran between the colliery and the New British Iron Company's ironworks for more than thirty years. The Plas Madoc branch trains also crossed the Pontcysyllte branch on the level at Plas-yn-Wern with traffic to and from Delph Brickworks, about two miles from the S & C.

South of the Dee: The Fron Branch

The importance of preparing fieldwork before going in search of lost railways was brought home to me when I went to survey the remains of the Fron branch, on the opposite bank of the Dee Valley from Ruabon. Whitehurst Halt was clearly marked on the latest edition of a map I had bought. It lay tucked away in a cutting beside the Holyhead Road—the A5. I arrived to find all had gone: just discernible was the course of a path down the embankment to the platforms on the S & C line. Yet the 1924 Divisional Report said that Whitehurst was an important exchange point in early days:

> . . . Coaches used to start from this point for all places in North Wales, e.g. Corwen, Carnarvon and Holyhead. At least one of the former early Superintendents of the Great Western Railway started his career at this station.

The Superintendent was not named, but the Report told me a lot about Whitehurst. There were shelters on both platforms, a lamp hut, and a small booking hut on the Up side. South of the A5 there were four sidings for 131 wagons, a 20-ton truck weighbridge, and a pen and loading bank for cattle on the Up side. The staff comprised a signalman (class 5); two signalmen (class 3); a porter-signalman and a lad porter, whose duties included trimming and lighting the oil lamps at Rhosymedre Halt, between Cefn and Ruabon. Traffic receipts in 1924 for so small and isolated a halt were impressive: £21,240, virtually all from general goods, bricks, lime, tarmac and timber. Buses competed for passengers, and the Shropshire Union canal (LMS-owned) was regarded as a freight competitor.

The station master controlled access to private sidings, Penybont, which served another of the brickworks owned by J. C. Edwards, and the Fron branch. Edwards' traffic was propelled into the siding and left inside a gate for collection by the firm's locomotive, which also brought traffic to the gate from the works, a little below in the Dee Valley.

On the opposite side of the S & C line, the Fron branch was gated and had a loop for eleven wagons. It ran west for ¾ mile to Chirk Castle Lime Works at Fron. It was worked by the GWR as part of the main line under an 1845 Agreement. The term 'worked' was perhaps a little misleading for Paddington could not tuck its engines into a tunnel under the SU Canal, and if it had they would not have got far, for Working Timetables stated: 'neither is the layout such as to enable engines to run to the Works'. This was a splendid understatement, as the lay-out consisted of two wagon turntables at either side of a narrow bridge carrying the line under the canal. Just after Grouping—when lime traffic was growing—a contractor was charging 4s 0d to handle each wagon each way between the Works and the Junction. The GWR thought that too much and was considering what to do.

In 1974, BR offered to sell the Fron branch to Wrexham Rural Council for £100; offering the Brymbo–Minera trackbed for £200 at the same time. By then, most of the Fron line had returned to nature, although its junction with the S & C line was just discernible where the grassy embankment dips between the site of Whitehurst Halt and the Dee viaduct.

Locomotive Workings

Rhos push-and-pull trains, which replaced steam railmotors, were worked by small tanks. Croes Newydd had a glorious assortment of them. Sometimes they seemed to lie in the back of the shed for weeks (I could never find them when I went spotting!). But when they were active they had to work hard. This was tank country—and no wonder! Gradients on the Pontcysyllte branch were tough: Rhos–Pant 1 in 54; Hughes & Lancaster's siding to Edwards' Works, 1 in 37; from there to Trevor station—a climb of 1 in 40 for southbound trains. In the final years before closure Croes Newydd kept two pannier tanks—Nos 1628/38—for working between Trevor and the Monsanto chemical works at Acrefair. Other routes around Ruabon were worked by panniers of the 16XX and 57XX classes and 0–6–2 tanks of the 56XX class.

CHAPTER 4

GWR Secondary

Towards the Coast

Because Grouping took place more than half a century ago it is easy to forget how small was the GWR foothold in North and Mid Wales until then. Besides the Shrewsbury & Chester line along the border and the short, though important, branches around Wrexham and Ruabon, the GWR owned only the secondary line from Ruabon to Dolgelley and the associated branch straggling the Arenig mountains to Blaenau Ffestiniog. Grouping changed all that, as by its takeover of the Cambrian Railways (the largest, though not the most prosperous of the Welsh companies), Paddington added 300 miles to its system. Almost one-third of that mileage consisted of the Cambrian main line between Whitchurch and Aberystwyth, which formed a second route to the Cambrian holiday coast complementary to the Dolgelley line, over which trains had reached Barmouth by running powers via Barmouth Junction. The history of the short, single line will be told in the Cambrian chapter because it was too important a part of that company's system to be considered merely as a vehicle of Paddington's coastal aspirations.

The takeover of the Cambrian, actually made in March 1922, as part of Grouping, made little difference to operating over the Ruabon line, which continued to be the shortest route between North West England and much of the holiday coast.

The Dolgelley and Ffestiniog lines are worthy of remembrance for their GWR connections. Besides being scenically beautiful, the Dolgelley route was historically more interesting than many lines for the mainly single line of $44\frac{1}{2}$ miles between Ruabon

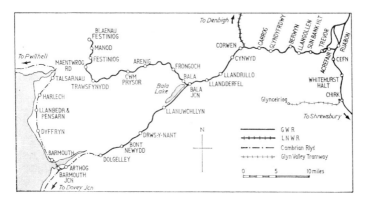

GWR secondary—Ruabon–Dolgelley, and over the hills to Blaenau
Ffestiniog

and Dolgelley was constructed by no fewer than four small
companies. They had close affinities and their destinies were
controlled without challenge by Paddington, with whom all
had working arrangements, since they owned neither locomotives nor stock.

The chairman of three of the companies was Henry Robertson, who did so much pioneering in the Wrexham area of
industry and railways. He believed that but for the GWRs
being a collector of minerals, many small coal mines would
have had to close for want of outlet.

At one time Paddington had high hopes of using the Dee
Valley lines to reach Aberystwyth, crossing the mountains via
the little Corris Railway, which was to be converted from
narrow to standard gauge and extended to the Dolgelley–Bala
section near Bontnewydd. The idea was soon forgotten, mainly
because of the extensive engineering works that it would have
involved, and the Great Western was also unsuccessful in its
opposition of extensions to the Aberystwyth & Welsh Coast
Railway. (See *The Cambrian Railways*, Vol 1, page 79.)

It so happened that the stretches each of slightly varying
length which were built by each company, matched small but

distinctive changes in the hilly and sometimes mountainous scenery. Construction was carried out westwards from the S & C line, which the GWR had taken over in 1854. It began modestly with the Vale of Llangollen Railway, incorporated five years later. The building of an easy $5\frac{1}{2}$ miles was accomplished without trouble, and from June 1862 tourists could reach the peace and beauty of Llangollen by rail. The branch took them through areas of contrasting scenery. At Ruabon (Llangollen Junction), the little trains swayed and rattled through a maze of small engineering, chemical and brickworks at Acrefair and Trevor, villages where terraces of houses shared with the railway the upper slopes of a hillside falling steeply into the Dee Valley.

Once through the smoky gauntlet, the trains continued a gentle descent to settle beside the river on the floor of the valley. Passengers caught glimpses of Pontcysyllte Aqueduct, which they no doubt supplemented with grandstand views once they had returned to Ruabon and were heading south for Shrewsbury over the Shrewsbury & Chester's splendid viaduct.

Llangollen lay close enough to Merseyside and Manchester quickly to become popular with day trippers and the branch from Ruabon was eventually doubled in late Victorian days (1898) to sidings reached via Llangollen Goods Junction. It lay nearly half a mile beyond the substantial station with an equally sturdy footbridge between the two curved platforms— the down one built on the edge of the shallow, rocky river. A goods yard was developed between the single line beyond the junction and the canal, a water-line branch of the Ellesmere fed from the Dee at Berwyn, about a mile away. Two groups of sidings could handle up to 300 wagons, although three were laid for stabling bank holiday specials. A fourth line ran to a canal wharf, where slates from a local quarry were transhipped for a period before Grouping. But this was not an area of industry, rather one of beauty. Those sidings, tucked away amid trees, were some of the least intrusive ever laid.

The railway itself slipped unobtrusively through Llangollen, once an important staging post on Telford's Holyhead road, which followed the opposite (south) bank of the river. Until 1865, tourists heading west towards Snowdonia and the coast had to take to that road. The Llangollen & Corwen Railway, second of the four companies, ran forward for ten miles and its plans, authorised in 1860 (a year after the Vale of Llangollen) provided for a route which kept close company with Telford's masterpiece, although the railway builders preferred a 689yd tunnel under a spur, rocky and wooded, that dominated the lower valley near Berwyn. There were no other major physical features to trouble the promoters en route to Corwen, although plenty of curves were necessary to keep clear of the river.

Junction at Corwen

The inhabitants of Corwen knew all about railways by the time the first train puffed in from Ruabon in May 1865, for the town since the previous autumn had been the terminus of the line from Denbigh and Ruthin in the neighbouring Vale of Clwyd, operated by a company in which Euston was much interested since it stemmed from its own system.

The Ruabon trains used a temporary terminus until, from September 1865, separate lines brought trains on each branch into a permanent station with waiting rooms on both platforms, and one for refreshments on the down. Such facilities (and extensive sidings) helped to make Corwen the largest intermediate station between Ruabon and Barmouth. After Grouping most of the 25 staff were employed jointly by the GWR and LMS, although, additionally, the GWR had a district inspector, three goods guards and half a signalman. The other $4\frac{1}{2}$ Corwen signalmen were jointly paid! The staff list made no mention of drivers for GWR buses (kept in a corrugated iron garage), which maintained services to the moorland village of Cerrig-y-Druidion, ten miles away on the A5, to Llandrillo, near Bala, on weekdays, and Llangollen on Sundays.

Corwen's third railway was the Corwen & Bala Railway,

49

incorporated in 1862 and the least spectacular, for it took railways into the flattish, broadening upper valley of the Dee. But the patchwork of green hills remained. The line was completed in two stages, to Llandrillo, in July 1866, and to Bala Old Station in May 1868. It was built from Corwen rather quicker than it had been from the east, and completion of the route between Ruabon and Dolgelley happened almost at once. Bala Old was a terminus for only a few weeks until the opening of the Bala & Dolgelly (*sic*) Railway on 4 August 1868. Paddington must have been satisfied to have reached the threshold of the Cambrian coast less than a year after the Cambrian had finished its coast line from Dovey Junction to Pwllheli in October 1867. However, a gap remained until the link-up at Dolgelley in 1869.

The B & D had been responsible for the longest link of the Ruabon route lifting it, in almost 18 miles, out of the Dee Valley, across the mountain watershed at Garneddwen and into the Wnion valley, where the river flowed west. Gradients were steep but not impossible, 1 in 58 at worst. And when one contemplates the hills, that was modest. The line's main role was as a through route, but between the world wars it enjoyed a fresh boost, as the GWR attempted to stimulate local, and to a certain extent, summer holiday traffic, by opening half-a-dozen more halts between 1928 and 1935. They brought the total of intermediate stations and halts between Ruabon and Barmouth Junction to 21—a large number for so sparsely populated an area.

The line never had enough freedom from the competition of the other three routes to the Cambrian coast to make it really prosperous. The Cambrian main line carried many holiday-makers from London and the Midlands, although those bound for Barmouth and places farther north often travelled on through coaches and trains via Ruabon. The Manchester & Milford route from Carmarthen also rivalled Ruabon's appeal, while that between Bangor and Afon Wen became tremendously busy for a time after the opening of Butlin's Holiday

Camp at Pwllheli. Once people preferred cars to trains, the sparsely-populated Cambrian coast could not hope to support four feeder lines, and Dr Beeching recommended that all but the Cambrian main line should be closed.

Closure was planned for mid-January 1965, but nature stepped in ahead of the economists and floods breached the single line near Llandderfel a month before and led to the closure of the through route. The section between Llangollen Goods Junction and Bala Junction was taken out of use and part-way passenger services maintained at either end. The same storms also severed the Manchester & Milford as a through route. It had been scheduled to close to passengers on the same day.

Paddington had encouraged people to use the line by its policy of providing halts. British Rail attempted the same thing in a different way by using it for sight-seeing trains. The Land Cruise trains, as they were known, ran under various titles from Festival of Britain year in 1951. Starting mainly from Rhyl they used a circular route via the Vale of Clwyd line to Corwen and then continued to Barmouth for a stop. The trains ran Mondays–Fridays (days when people were staying in North Wales) and did not present problems by interfering with the Saturday holiday traffic.

Ghosts and Vandals

Trains and track were made to disappear convincingly enough once closure decisions were taken, but many stations have remained—stationary. The beauty of the mountains and sea make even half-closed, half-derelict Barmouth Junction (Morfa Mawddach since 1960) seem as out of place as a lump of putty on a diamond ring. A mercifully-placed embankment hides to most tourists the true extent of vandalism to Dolgelley station, but it is a disturbing sight to anyone who walks over the pleasant bridge across the river Wnion.

The railway has left behind other problems. In 1974, a

51

Corwen councillor was critical of councils offering farmers un-
wanted parts of the old trackbed. Its purchase had been a great
boon to those who loved walking through the countryside. He
wrote to the *Liverpool Daily Post*: 'Children play merrily, young
and old walk happily away from cars and the invading crowds.'

Bala Lake Railway

Local councils took up the option to buy the entire trackbed
and one result has been the development of a quite charming
narrow gauge line, the Bala Lake Railway. From the carriage
window just west of Bala Junction, Victorian tourists enjoyed
in comfort the sort of scenery that they lapped up usually only
in guide book sketches. Beside them was the southern shore of
the lake and beyond, stretching away to the sky, scenery wild,
remote and rugged. The final backcloth was provided by the
shapely Arenig mountains. The creation of the modest 2ft 0in
gauge Bala Lake Railway has given back to the tourist who has
time to contemplate, the pleasure and inspiration that is to be
drawn from that view across the lake. The first stretch of the
little railway was opened in August 1972 from Llanuwchllyn
station (880330). The original line served that village and
Llangower Park and district. A GWR Chester Division report
of 1924 noted: 'It is stated that this was the first place in the
British Isles to be lighted by electricity.' That is one assertion
which, as a railway historian, I have no knowledge to confirm
or deny. But at Grouping the station was lit by oil. It was a
busy enough rural outpost with a crossing loop and a pleasant
signal box, with its back to the lake. It is all there still, for
although narrow gauge track has replaced the former layout,
it is still controlled from the signal box. The Bala Lake Railway
ran in its opening season to Llangower Halt (originally opened
10 June 1929) and at the time of writing was being extended
progressively eastwards towards Bala.

The stretch it uses may not prove to be the only one to be
revived, for in 1974 a group of enthusiasts announced more

Page 53 (Above) Dolgellau, looking east, in 1963. The station buildings included a footwarmers room.

(Below) Carrog, a wayside station of massive proportions, situated in glorious countryside in the middle of nowhere.

Page 54 Over the mountains – 1. *(Above)* Bala, ¾-mile from Bala Junction, was the first station on the Blaenau Ffestiniog branch. In this view, taken in 1958, ex-GWR pannier tank 4617 waits with the 15.40 local as far as Trawsfynydd, and 4645 heads the 14.20 Blaenau Ffestiniog – Bala Junction.

(Below) In the mountain bowl. No. 7443 at Cwm Prysor Halt in 1956 on the 15.40 local from Bala Junction.

ambitious plans for a standard gauge revival. One of the new district councils had talks with the Flint & Deeside Railway Preservation Society about re-opening another attractive section between Llangollen and Corwen, with a possible later extension to Bala. Following the discussions, the Society began a feasibility study. Meanwhile the Clwyd Planning Officer, Mr Colin Jacobs, reported in September 1974 on a Society proposal to re-open Llangollen station and three miles of track to the west. The cost of station restoration and relaying the first mile was put at £60,000. The report stated that the operators of the eight small railways in Wales were 'understandably apprehensive' about the prospect of competition, but it pointed out that three of the eight lines were already pushing ahead with their own expansion and restoration schemes. It was considered that a railway at Llangollen would become a major tourist attraction in the Dee Valley which would have more than 100,000 visitors a year. Clwyd Planning and Amenities Committees approved in principle the restoration of steam and agreed to lease Llangollen station and part of the trackbed towards Corwen to the F & D RPS for five years at a nominal rent. But late in 1974 the plan was threatened by a request to the local authority from the Welsh Office to safeguard several routes proposed for the A5 by-pass at Llangollen. They include one which would prevent the restoration of the line. And a developer became interested in using the station site for an hotel.

The Preservation Society also doubted whether a line could reach Corwen because a fire station is likely to be built on the trackbed just east of the station. It would mean a new station would have to be built about half a mile from the town.

But difficulties have not proved deterrents to the enthusiasts who are forging ahead with plans despite the uncertainty of the by-pass route, still to be decided. Llangollen station was 're-opened' (with a diesel and single length of rail) on 13 September 1975 after several months of intensive clearance work by the Group, which also needs to clear and relay $3\frac{1}{2}$ miles of track and raise £150,000—this much-increased sum on initial estimates is due to inflation.

Providing a tourist attraction and finding a use for Llangollen station, which the *Liverpool Daily Post* described as a 'legacy of dereliction', pleases everyone, enthusiasts and councils alike, and the planners say that the by-pass (which might not affect the railway), is unlikely to be completed before 1985.

CHAPTER 5

GWR Mountain

Bala–Blaenau Ffestiniog

'The Rail route from Bala to Festiniog (*sic*) is probably the wildest and most impressive hour of rail travelling in England or Wales.' Bradley's comment in 1908 had been true from the opening of the line a quarter of a century earlier, and was to remain so up to closure half a century later. That closure took place in 1961, partly to make way for a spectacular development and landscape change, the creation of the Tryweryn Reservoir in the Arenig hills (mountains, really) north of Bala. It may be claimed that while the Ruabon–Barmouth Junction route was the most important of the Forgotten Railways of North Wales (with Bangor–Afon Wen a close second), the Ffestiniog route was the most glorious. The very spirit of the lonely mountains breathed through the official jargon of working timetables. Note a Chester Division Report, again 1924:

> At Cwm Prysor, midway between Arenig and Trawsfynydd, the line is 1,200 feet above sea level and on clear days Snowdon can be seen.

Cwm Prysor halt lay at twice the height above sea level as Bala. Nearby was the major engineering work—a curved viaduct, over which the first train passed, from the Bala side, on 29 July 1882—four months ahead of the opening to Ffestiniog.

Many winters there was snow a-plenty, as Appendix No 14 to the GWR Service timetable freely acknowledged:

> Should the weather indicate a heavy fall of snow during the

night such as is likely to break down the telegraph communication on the section between Arenig and Trawsfynydd, the
Station Masters at Arenig and Trawsfynydd, after the last train
of the day has passed, and before leaving duty, will communi-
cate with each other, and, if they consider it necessary, are
hereby authorised to withdraw an electric token from the
instrument at Arenig to enable the snow plough to pass over
the section the following morning.

From the Dolgelley line at Bala Junction, the Ffestiniog line
ran three-quarters of a mile to a station serving the small but
important town of Bala (with respectable passenger receipts in
1924 of £4,566). The two-platform station and the nearby
engine shed were conventional enough, but the 38ft long goods
shed was splendidly original. It was built with turrets and
looked like a mock castle, a design insisted on by a landowner
who opposed the railway.

From Bala the branch climbed steadily up a narrowing
valley to Arenig, a busy quarry village, where there were sidings for a hundred wagons and annual mineral receipts reached
five figures. From Cwm Prysor, three miles beyond, the line
dropped towards Trawsfynydd, 17 miles from Bala Junction.
The sectional Appendix was full of notes about Trawsfynydd,
and listed a long code of whistles and crows that sometimes
echoed on the mountain breezes, used by locomotives shunting
in the troop yard, built just beyond the station to handle traffic
for a large artillery camp opened in 1903. The troop yard had
its own platforms, both more than 450ft long. One narrowed
for about half its length to provide a gun platform and end-on
dock. Troop trains were usually double-headed and special
instructions applied:

> An experienced Guard, well acquainted with the Bala and
> Blaenau Ffestiniog line, must in all cases work in charge of the
> troop trains, both loaded and empty, between Bala and
> Trawsfynydd.

Another joy of writing about this line, apart from evoking

personal memories, is that at Trawsfynydd it ceases to be a forgotten railway, for the five miles north to Blaenau Ffestiniog are used by trains carrying waste from Trawsfynydd nuclear power station, sent to Windscale works in Cumbria via Llandudno Junction. At Blaenau Ffestiniog they use a connection put in after the branch to Bala closed, to join the northern tip of the Conway Valley line, built by the LNWR, which tunnelled for more than two miles to reach the town.

Personal memories of the route include an early spring trip with a nuclear waste train when a bitterly cold wind was funnelled up the Vale of Festiniog and caught the mountain flank to which the line clings all the way. As we propelled from Blaenau Ffestiniog, we kept warm by jumping off the brake van and chasing dozens of newly-born lambs off the track. The stretch from Blaenau Ffestiniog runs through Llan Ffestiniog, a village that was the southern outpost of the Snowdonia slate quarrying industry. Originally the two centres were joined by a narrow gauge line, the Festiniog & Blaenau, opened in 1868 by quarry owners wanting access to the sea via the Festiniog Railway, which had also established interchange sidings with the Cambrian Railways at Minffordd the previous year. This was then the nearest standard gauge line, for the Conway Valley branch was not complete.

From the start, the F & B provided for conversion from narrow to standard gauge to join the Merionethshire Railway, incorporated to run 10 miles from the Cambrian at Talsarnau. That line was forgotten before it could be remembered! But the F & B was converted to standard gauge in 1883 following the opening of the line from Bala as far as Llan Ffestiniog nearly a year earlier. The line was the fourth to reach Blaenau Ffestiniog and like the others (two narrow gauge), its promoters were attracted by slate traffic. Yet although the line from Bala would geographically seem to be the shortest between Snowdonia and the Midlands, it offered little saving in mileage, primarily because of the Ruabon–Barmouth Junction route running due east.

Apart from a siding with gantry for lifting atomic containers on and off lorries at Trawsfynydd, the line from Blaenau Ffestiniog is now single beyond the town goods yard. It bisects the waste land of the once-busy GWR yard which could hold up to 150 wagons. GWR locomotives used to run half a mile south to turn at a shed tucked into the hillside at Tanymanod. That, too, has gone, but at Manod there is visible a trace of the original narrow gauge route.

The Bala line closed to passengers in 1960 with a memorable Stephenson Locomotive Society special, which two pannier tanks had difficulty in hauling, and to goods in January 1961. The route, so interesting in life, remains so in death. Closure took place not only because freight traffic was sparse, but also because near Frongoch Halt the track lay on land essential to the creation of Tryweryn Reservoir, stretching nearly two miles, on which Liverpool spent £20,000,000 to supplement the water supply that the city takes from Vyrnwy. Diverting the branch to higher ground (for which powers were obtained) would have cost another million pounds and closure followed an agreement with Liverpool Corporation to bear the cost of the new connection at Blaenau Ffestiniog. Local people fought hard to save the Bala locals, pointing out that in the previous season (1959) another railway in the hills of Merioneth had carried 76,000 passengers. By then, however, the Festiniog Railway was better situated to be a tourist attraction. Those little trains will never match the echoes once heard on the Bala branch as troop trains, sometimes headed by two class 43XX Moguls, stormed their way to Trawsfynydd. Occasionally, Manors took a hand, but on the normal passenger trains, pannier tanks were the bread-and-butter locomotives. They were kept busy, for besides the heavy gradients and wintry weather they were booked to call at eight stations and have enough steam in hand to restart from up to seven halts on demand. The through service of three daily trains each way was supplemented by workmen's locals at either end of the route: between Bala and Arenig, and Trawsfynydd and Blaenau Ffestiniog. And there was a local shuttle service between Bala and Bala Junction. These days, even when the area is crowded with summer holidaymakers it seems remote and it remains hard to recall that it once enjoyed such comparatively intensive local passenger services. The dam at the eastern end of the Tryweryn Reservoir offers a lofty perch from which to view what was the approach of the humble branch line up a valley into the mountains. And there are a host (almost a feast) of other remains to enjoy: Cwm Prysor's shapely viaduct and the ledge on which the railway reached it from the west. It ran high above the Bala road and looking up the bare mountainside one may be forgiven for wondering just how trains managed to cling to it and never fall into the valley so far below.

CHAPTER 6

GWR by Adoption

Cambrian Delights

There is so much of the Cambrian Railways still alive to enjoy (from Welshpool down the Severn Valley and through the hills to the glorious coast stretching for miles between Aberystwyth and Pwllheli) that it is hard to realise how much has gone. Inland, Welshpool lies at the end of a main line that once stretched another 34 miles through Oswestry to Whitchurch. Four of those miles survive between Oswestry and Llynclys Junction which form part of a route to Nantmawr stone and gravel quarries from which BR at times collect ballast. The section is fed by the GWR branch from Gobowen, and includes part of the former Tanat Valley Light Railway.

The Cambrian was a line of 'bits' hence its official title Cambrian Railways being plural. Typically, two sections made up the Welshpool–Whitchurch leg; the Oswestry & Newtown Railway built the 16 miles between Welshpool and Oswestry, while the other 18 were developed by the Oswestry, Ellesmere & Whitchurch Railway.

The essentially and proudly Welsh nature of the Cambrian did not prevent it establishing its headquarters in the best place it could find. Dismissing claims by the people of Welshpool, it chose Oswestry and the Shropshire town grew to be one of the most distinctive of what may now be called the forgotten railway towns of Britain, which became the hubs of important and quite extensive railways that retained their independence until grouping. (Another example was Melton Constable on the Midland & Great Northern in North Norfolk.) The small railway towns were never so famous as Swindon, Crewe or Doncaster, but always they were busy and fascinating, sometimes charming—qualities they gained from lying off the beaten track.

At Oswestry steam was everywhere. It poured from locomotives out-shopped after spells inside the whitewashed walls of the works; from others at the substantial shed in the fork between the diverging Gobowen and Whitchurch lines; from locomotives shunting in the large goods yard bounded by the station, shed and works, and in a small yard tucked away at the south end of the station. Steam marked the main line comings and goings of expresses, mails and goods, and of fussy little locals from Llanfyllin, a market town in the rolling hills to the west, and the Tanat Valley.

The first steam sighted at Oswestry was that of the Shrewsbury & Chester Railway, when it mildly established its presence in 1848 with a single-track 2½-mile branch from Gobowen (where the Italianate station is an architectural gem that ought not to be missed).

Second to reach Oswestry was the Oswestry & Newtown, which arrived from the opposite direction after an interval of 12 years and three years later began building its locomotive and carriage works, housed in an impressive building, mostly single storey, stretching just over 800ft and 'squashed' between the main line and a green round-topped hill, which the *Gossiping Guide to Wales* encouraged tourists to climb to get a grandstand view above the rooftop:

> I think it would be worth your while, to gain an idea of the architecture and proportion of the whole pile of buildings, to ascend the slopes of Old Oswestry, and then you will allow, I think, that though the workshops seldom improve the appearance of a place, these add to, rather than detract from, the beauty of Oswestry, as seen from that spot, while the chimney, octagon in shape, 150 feet high, is a prominent object in the landscape for miles around.

Works apart (for they are still used by industrial firms),

Oswestry has disposed of its marks as a railway town more surely than most of the system it served. Half the station has been demolished and the yard lifted, but a preservation society began to be active in 1973 so all may not be lost. But Oswestry will not easily forget the Cambrian, and the Victorian prosperity that it brought. Again, the *Gossiping Guide* of 1879:

> Whilst many small towns have been damaged by the introduction of railways, Oswestry has wholly benefitted; its trade has increased, its borders are enlarged, its shops have improved, and there is a greater air of business about its inhabitants.

Today, the scene has changed and Oswestry's appearance has been badly damaged by the virtual disappearance of railways. Only a single line (from Gobowen to Nantmawr, via Llynclys Junction) threads the derelict station area. Occasional trains run to collect stone from the Nantmawr quarries. The quite modern GWR shed, which lay in the fork of the Gobowen and Whitchurch lines, has been enclosed and extended for industrial use. The Cambrian locomotive and carriage works is occupied by private firms, including Davies & Metcalfe of Romiley, the railway equipment makers who supplied the Cambrian Railways. The works retains the original locomotive weather vane and the Cambrian footbridge across the once extensive track layout remains, too.

In 1974, signal boxes at both ends of the Cambrian station lay derelict. The long, two-storey building on the down platform and the substantial footbridge had been demolished, while the building on the up platform (the main headquarters of the Cambrian Railways) was part-vandalised and part-used by a newspaper group, which has its main offices across the road. Platform edges crumble, but beside the bay on the main one a corrugated iron cycle shed remains, with its notice stating: 'This cycle shed is for the use of operating and commercial staff only.' A decade ago bicycles were real—I remember seeing them as I climbed off the footplate of a Manor class locomotive on which I had travelled from Aberystwyth.

Oswestry has a Manor again, *Foxcote Manor* (1950–66), delivered to enthusiasts of the Cambrian Railways Society Limited, who bought it from Barry for £4,950, on 11 January 1975. They hope to steam it on the Nantmawr line from their headquarters in the Cambrian goods yard and shed at the south end of the station, which is still connected to the mineral line. The enthusiasts' hopes received a boost with the re-opening to steam in 1975 of the Shrewsbury & Chester line. The Cambrian yard is neat and tidy so perhaps we may look forward to a modest and pleasant rebirth of the steam age at Oswestry.

South of Oswestry, the line to Welshpool ran into the broad Severn Valley following the pleasant, though unspectacular west bank for several miles. Passengers enjoyed noble views of the craggy Briedden Hill on the far bank. Llanymynech, most important of the intermediate stations, served no more than a village, but once it was a junction for the rather eccentric Shropshire & Montgomery, whose passenger trains from Shrewsbury reached its own platforms at Llanymynech fitfully through the years.

Oswestry, Ellesmere & Whitchurch Railway

The OE & W was alien to most of the Cambrian in two senses. Geographically it ran mostly in England, skirting an isolated part of the County of Flint en route between its two Shropshire terminals. Physically, too the line was different, as the countryside through which it ran was distinctly flatter than much of the territory of the Cambrian, of which it was one of the four original constituents. The Cambrian Railways was formed on 25 July 1864 and two days later the OE & W was opened to complete the main line between Whitchurch and Aberystwyth.

The OE & W was, like all the main line, more of a through route than one serving small areas. Despite the flattish Shropshire countryside, the OE & W was not an easy line to build, mainly because of a three-mile bog known as Whixall Moss.

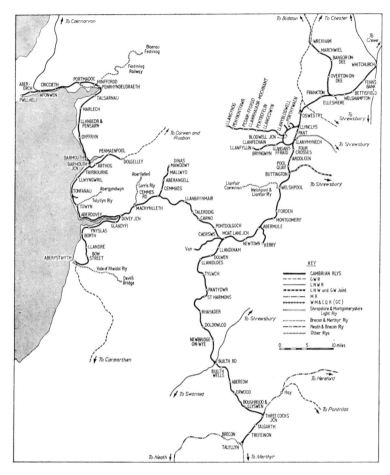

The Cambrian Railways—a lot has gone, but much of what was the biggest of the independent Welsh railways survives

The contractors adopted much the same methods as George Stephenson had done to take the Liverpool & Manchester across Chat Moss, sinking a raft of brushwood to support the track in the absence of firm foundations. Whittington station near Oswestry, where the line bridged the Shrewsbury & Chester, grew into an interchange with platforms at each level, but was never much used. Far busier was a neighbouring halt on the Whitchurch route—Tinker's Green opened in 1939 to serve a large Army camp at Park Hall.

Tourists know the little intermediate town of Ellesmere as a pleasant spot for picnics, to be relished beside tree-shaded meres. Railway (and social) historians know Ellesmere well because the station master became famous in trade union history. After John Hood was sacked in 1892, Parliament took note and several Cambrian directors were censured before the Bar of the House of Commons for breach of privilege. (*The Cambrian Railways*, Vols 1 and 2.) Hood never tried to rejoin the Cambrian after the fuss died down, but he continued to live in Ellesmere until he died in 1920 in a house that he bought with money collected by people who thought the Cambrian had given him a raw deal. They admired his courage in speaking in defence of a porter sacked through no fault of his own. The station building that Hood knew is still there but its surroundings are different, as the building has been incorporated into an industrial estate developed in recent years that takes in the entire station yard. A more visually satisfying station to see is Frankton, tucked away in a cutting in the middle of nowhere. It is a private house but from the lane beside one can get a good view of the Cambrian coat of arms in the gable end. It is believed Frankton was so endowed because it was the residence of a senior officer of the Cambrian. More road-accessible is Welshampton station, now also private. It lies beside a hump bridge over the trackbed carrying the Whitchurch–Oswestry main road.

Wrexham & Ellesmere Railway

Three years after Hood left Ellesmere, it became a junction with the arrival in winter 1895 of the Wrexham & Ellesmere Railway. Several times I resolved to travel over the 13-mile single line but to my lasting regret, never did. It was a route that prodded tentatively at Wrexham's heart.

Cambrian trains, which worked the line from the start, never

CAMBRIAN RAILWAYS
Tourist Arrangements

C.S. DENNISS.
SECRETARY. & GEN. MANAGER.

1905

May 1ˢᵗ
ᴛᴏ June 30ᵀᴴ

Seventy years later: a Cambrian Railways brochure tells of so much
that has gone

got beyond Central, but that was not too serious a setback for they were able to make connections with WM & CQ locals, and Central was on the doorstep of Wrexham's busy shopping centre. Some trains that used the single line between Wrexham and Ellesmere did roam beyond Central, for hundreds of miles. The $12\frac{3}{4}$ miles were part of a tenuous chain exploited by the Great Central to push expresses from cities and towns on its system as far south as Leicester through to the Welsh coast. What a long journey it must have been—from Leicester north to Sheffield and through Woodhead to Manchester and thence via Chester. Somebody must have felt it worthwhile, for at Ellesmere a spur was laid to allow the expresses to reach Oswestry without reversal. The Wrexham & Ellesmere is an almost totally uninteresting lost railway. A section survives from Wrexham to serve a local trading estate. Once I ran over it on a special but the line and its scenery provided no stimulation. Ghosts had been truly laid. Local stations, since demolished, were vandalised ruins.

But lest the valediction be too harsh, it must be remembered that the Wrexham & Ellesmere enabled a company, in addition to the Great Central, to achieve useful things. It allowed the Cambrian (which worked, but never absorbed the company), to reach Wrexham. Did that matter? It was important to the Cambrian, for Wrexham was the largest town that it served. Many years later, during World War II, the line really came into its own, providing access to a large Royal Ordnance Factory developed near Sesswick Halt at the Wrexham end of the branch. It had its own railway system that grew to some four miles and part was used by workers' specials. After the war the ROF was replaced by an industrial estate whose factories relied far less on rail. By 1960 all that remained was a half-mile stretch to a gas works, and operated as a siding.

Wrexham Central was a place where tank engines rubbed shoulders. In latter days, GWR 0–4–2 tanks, which had charge of the one-coach Ellesmere motor trains, came to rest in a platform close to the more stately Robinson C13s. At Ellesmere, the little tanks would wait patiently as Whitchurch–Aberystwyth trains roared by, 4-4-0s in charge in Cambrian days, Manors, together with several of the smaller BR standard types in final years. Cambrian locomotives often spent hours at Whitchurch because there were no balanced workings for immediate turn-round, or because expresses from the LNWR were running late. The Cambrian achieved little in the way of speed in Shropshire, but over the flatter stretch between Oswestry and Welshpool, expresses often managed their best point-to-point timings; averages were low—around 37mph.

Tanat Valley Light Railway

Occasionally, history tells us, a fisherman or two caught a train at Llanymynech and travelled over the Nantmawr branch as far as Blodwell Junction, where they would step on to the short platform. The view that greeted them was delightful but the sight of a little Tanat Valley connection must have been welcome, for the junction was in the middle of fields and so, mainly, were the rest of the stations that were established in the valley. Yet the Tanat was a splendid place in which to fish and 'get away from it all'. From the start, guide books proclaimed it as little-known. Baddeley stated in 1904 (the line had opened that January):

> This little line traverses an extremely pretty valley, and affords
> a most welcome access to a very picturesque part of the country,
> which, but for the exceptional attraction of Pistyll Rhayadr has
> hitherto been but little known to the tourist.

The line had its terminus in the lead mining village of Llangynog at the foot of the Berwyns, but had the early pro-moters got their way the station, which lay a little distance from the village, might have had a different role. A scheme of 1860 would have placed it on the through route of the West Midlands, Shrewsbury & Coast of Wales Railway. Once the enor-

Page 71 Over the mountains – 2. *(Above)* Maentwrog Road was the station for Tanybwlch, but the village was three miles away, as the station nameboard clearly proclaimed.

(Below) Blaenau Ffestiniog GWR terminus was modest, but it was an interchange with the Festiniog Railway.

Page 72 Cambrian Railways. *(Above)* On 11 January 1965 the SLS Farewell to Oswestry, Ellesmere and Whitchurch leaves Oswestry behind ex-GWR 4-6-0 No 7802 *Bradley Manor*.

(Below) Llanfyllin was closed at the same time. Pictured here in 1962 is 2-6-0 46509 on the 15.45 from Oswestry.

mous cost of tunnelling the Berwyns was realised, no further schemes for a through route were seriously considered, but in their wake came a host of schemes for branch lines to open up the valley.

The quarry branch that remains to Nantmawr takes trains (on part of the morning pick-up freight diagram from Shrewsbury) to within sight of the derelict platform of Blodwell Junction. That was the starting point of the line that was built— the Tanat Valley Light Railway. The rest of the route followed by the little local trains to and from Oswestry was over Cambrian metals. The Tanat was built under a Light Railway Order of 1899 which although it eased constructional requirements, did not help financially. A grant came from the Treasury and financial help from several local authorities, but still money was short. The Cambrian made a working agreement, but it was not until 1904 that the Tanat appeared in the company's timetables, although it was said that several trains had taken local people to market at Oswestry before then.

The Light Railway Commissioners considered two schemes before making their decision. The other was for a narrow gauge of 2ft 6in (the same as the Welshpool & Llanfair) from Llanfyllin. An attractive line as that would have been bound to have caught the eye of preservationists and steam might still have been found in the Tanat Valley. As it was, when the time came for closure of the standard gauge line, there was nothing special to commend it for revival. Traffic was withdrawn in three stages. Passenger services stopped temporarily when the nation was short of coal in winter 1951, but they were never restored and their official withdrawal date some 18 months later coincided with the closure of the upper section completely beyond Llanrhaiadr Mochnant. The remaining section from there to Blodwell Junction was closed in the winter of 1960 after floods damaged a bridge.

It is perhaps worth remembering that the Tanat was the third light railway to open in Wales within a three-year period. The Vale of Rheidol in 1902 was followed a year later by the

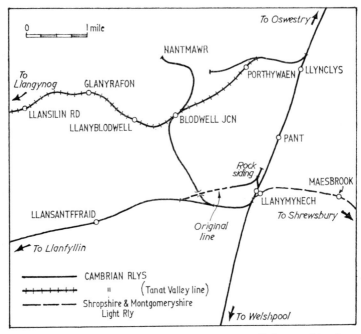

Border Country—an extravagance of lines, Gobowen–Llynclys–
Nantmawr being the sole remnant

From the 1905 brochure—the Tanat remains largely untrodden, but
motorists know it

Welshpool & Llanfair, serving the same Border country as the Tanat—then and now!

The Llanfyllin Railway

Lesser known, yet equally distinctive, for several reasons, possibly through being built by small independent companies on local initiative; possibly because of antiquated rolling stock and operating methods, were lines which eventually merged to become short Cambrian branches. One which formed part of the Cambrian from its creation was almost brand new at that time: the Llanfyllin Railway, opened in 1865 by the Oswestry & Newtown Railway. The pleasant green Border country through which it ran to give the busy market town a 'with it' artery with the outside world, more especially Oswestry, had long been considered for conquest by rail promoters.

Between its opening and closure in 1965 (at the same time as the Oswestry–Welshpool main line section), it underwent only one improvement, but that was rather radical. This was carried out in 1896 to avoid the local trains having to reverse in the middle of their journey. At the approach to the junction at Llanymynech, a short connection was made to the branch from Llanymynech to Nantmawr, part of a line opened from Shrewsbury (Abbey Foregate) by the Potteries, Shrewsbury & North Wales Railways—the famous 'Potts'—in 1866 and closed soon afterwards. It ailed for years and at the instigation of a quarry owner the Cambrian took over working the section of the then bankrupt 'Potts' between Llanymynech and Nantmawr from 1881. When Colonel Stephens revived the 'Potts' in 1909, the Cambrian kept him off the branch because it pointed out that it had worked the branch for years when there was no one else about to do so.

With the Welshpool & Llanfair so close, there is the temptation to forget the scanty remains of the Tanat and Llanfyllin branches and spend all the time available indulging in Welsh and perhaps Continental nostalgia which the little railway provides. Yet to do that would be to miss savouring the erstwhile flavour of the two standard gauge lines. The Llanfyllin terminus retains its station buildings and goods shed, now merged for commercial use, so it is easy to visualise how much more substantial was railway development to serve this market town than at Llanfair Caereinion.

Motorists using the Oswestry–Dolgellau road (A495) now find that a once-sharp bend at the west end of Llansaintffraid has been eased, partly by using the railway trackbed. In the village itself they find, looking perhaps a little out of place, the very obvious goods shed. It lies beside a small car park. There is also the station, which has been turned into a restaurant and the buildings extended.

There has not been the pressure for extensive trackbed utilisation in the Tanat Valley, but development is taking place slowly. In 1974 the station yard at Penybontfawr was offered for sale with planning permission for four bungalows.

Kerry Branch

It is far easier to write factually about Abermule as the scene of one of the most noted railway accidents in history, than as the junction of a branch that was among the loveliest in Wales. For my words cannot match the pleasure I always feel when I am in the area. Kerry lies on the hills on the south side of the narrowing Severn Valley. It is a scattered community of sheep farmers and it was John Wilkes, the first breeder of the famous Kerry sheep, who was responsible for the short branch. He pressed for a railway to carry sheep and farm produce at a time when the Oswestry & Newtown was completing its twisting single line through the valley.

The rising hillside was too steep for a line to climb, but there was the deep gorge of the river Mule, and it was found possible to push a line, twisting and steeply graded (1 in 43), to the rolling hilly countryside above. In days before total closure in 1956 the branch goods was worked by one of the last Dean

0–6–0s, No 2516, now at the Swindon Museum. On wet days the goods was often cancelled, as the rails were too greasy for the locomotive to get a proper grip. One of the tiny stations was at Fronfraith, half way up, where an overbridge (still extant) had two arches of contrasting size; the smaller spanned the tumbling river, the other was tailor-built to accommodate the single line, though only just for the clearance was very restricted. Kerry was the interchange point until about 1922 for a narrow gauge steam tramway that spreadeagled across the hills from the little terminus to serve the sheep farms and forestry plantations.

Mid Wales Railway

There are few lines over which I travelled only once (and in only one direction), that haunt my mind in the way that do memories of the Mid Wales Railway. Here surely was an almost perfect secondary line offering almost everything to the passengers—notably the pastoral Wye and its surrounding hills, though the Kyle of Lochalsh line still offers an even finer variety of mountain scenery and (joy of joys) the prospect of the Isles and the sea.

Trains on the Mid Wales Railway ran between the Cambrian main line at Moat Lane and Brecon, but for several miles at each end they used rails that were not part of the original system. For the MWR ran from Llanidloes, southern terminus of the pioneer Llanidloes & Newtown Railway, to Talyllyn, where it joined the Brecon & Merthyr and used running powers to reach Brecon itself.

The MWR never achieved the traffic that its promoters hoped for because it had several bigger and better-placed competitors. The Cambrian Railways was the biggest independent system in Wales and the Mid Wales became one of its longest limbs. It was vulnerable to competition from lines that were more direct and could handle more traffic. To the east lay the Shrewsbury & Hereford and, much farther west, the

Manchester & Milford, which captured part of the holiday traffic between South Wales and Aberystwyth. Competition was marginally extended by the construction of the Central Wales Railway.

Remoteness was the essence of the Mid Wales line, most noticeable at junctions like Talyllyn and Three Cocks, near Brecon, at Moat Lane, near Newtown, and at Builth Road. All were virtually in the middle of nowhere, yet each had refreshment rooms. Moat Lane station rose to three storeys with steep gables and lofty chimney pots: splendid, if uninspired architecture. What wide views of the Severn Valley and the rolling hills its windows commanded!

Moat Lane was not as pleasant a station as that at Llanidloes, Georgian in style, better proportioned with large bay windows, symbolic of a more leisurely age. Whitehall has been dragged into the fight to save it from demolition to make way for the main road to South Wales. A public inquiry into objections to the station demolition was held at Llanidloes on 4 June 1974, when it was stated that much of the by-pass would be built on the MWR trackbed. The road would not actually go through the station, but the buildings would have to be demolished to give traffic visibility. A senior official of the Royal Commission on Ancient Monuments in Wales said that the station had been part of the grandeur of the railway age and was the finest Victorian building in Llanidloes. It could be used as a public building.

Llanidloes lay at the southern end of the most historic section of the Mid Wales route, for the line between there and Newtown was built by the Llanidloes & Newtown, incorporated in 1853 as the first railway in Mid Wales. The Mid Wales Railway was authorised in 1859–60 as the culmination of schemes for a through route from Milford Haven (one of the nearest British ports to America) to Lancashire. The original aim was to carry cotton to Lancashire and its industrial goods for export.

The most famous of the schemes was that of the Manchester & Milford, which managed to construct 44 miles of line northwards from Carmarthen. The main obstacle to further progress (apart from a chronic money shortage) was the great mass of Plynlimon, separating West Wales from the Severn Valley. It was to be tunnelled as part of a 50-mile section between Llanidloes and Pencader. After it was authorised in 1860 it was realised that the section from Llanidloes to Penpontbren, where the line was to branch west into the mountains, would duplicate the route of the MWR. Neither company could agree about which should construct and run the section—a mere $1\frac{1}{2}$ miles in length—and the Llanidloes & Newtown was asked to do so instead. Only three miles west from Penpontbren to the village of Llangurig were ever built, being completed in 1864.

The section was laid with double track (in readiness for the L & N to Llanidloes being improved), but only the down track was used. And apart from contractor's trains, only one goods is known to have reached Llangurig. This was a pity, for the journey beyond there on the projected M & M would have been very exciting. Soon after leaving the village, the train would have been in a long tunnel (on which construction actually began); out of that and into another, and before reaching the coastal plain of West Wales it would have crossed a viaduct 280ft high. High hopes of such wonders in the hills lingered for years. On two winter nights in January 1872 meetings were held in the Public Rooms at Llanidloes to support the idea of the Llangurig branch being extended to Aberystwyth. But after the audience dispersed, the concept seemed to as well.

The MWR maintained a limited interest in the fortunes of the M & M, as it was anxious to use a branch that was projected from its mountain route at Devil's Bridge to Aberystwyth. When it became obvious that nothing would come of this branch, the MWR forgot its coastal aspirations and attempted to force passage into the mining valleys of South Wales, only to be thwarted, totally, by the Brecon & Merthyr, authorised the same day. There were several bitter squabbles among companies seeking access to Brecon, including the ancient Hay Railway and the Hereford, Hay & Brecon, destined to become part of the Midland Railway and share tracks with the Cambrian beyond Three Cocks.

The MWR also joined the LNWR at Builth Road by a curving single-line spur from the Central Wales line, of which traces remain. Builth Road High Level lost its suffix after the MWR line closed in 1962. From the dmus that still call, passengers can get a good view of the changes that have taken place at Low Level, where the station buildings remain but the platforms have been flattened and the trackbed extensively used for agricultural industry.

Elan Valley Railway

The Llangurig branch was not the only one stemming from the Mid Wales Railway to become forgotten a long time ago. There was another which had a rather more busy and useful life—a line that owed its short existence to expansion by Birmingham many miles away.

The Elan Valley Railway was completely private, being developed and worked by Birmingham Corporation Waterworks Department, during the construction of four major dams in the valley. Eventually the line grew to some seven miles and it was opened in 1894 from the MWR just south of Rhayader; interchange sidings were established near the junction at Noyadd. During the next 12 years workmen's trains ran on the system, although they never strayed onto the Mid Wales. The system provided the Cambrian with useful goods revenue, yet when it closed in 1917 the Cambrian may have welcomed the end of the traffic. By then the Mid Wales route was enjoying an importance it had never had before, and would never have again as one of the routes used by the Jellicoe Specials, carrying coal from South Wales to the Grand Fleet at Scapa. By night and day, seven days a week, those trains kept the Mid Wales open.

The locomotives used were small—Cambrian 0-6-0s; the track would not stand bigger. Even in GWR days locomotives bigger than a Dean six-coupled were barred from running south of Llanidloes because of weight restrictions, but in final years LMS standard 6400 class Moguls dominated traffic.

The Van Railway

Just after the Battle of Britain, when the country stood almost alone and many events were veiled in wartime secrecy, news was given of the closure of the little Van Railway, another line (although developed independently) that also ran from the Severn Valley into the hills. Actually there was no need to hush up this economy of winter 1940 for it was really nothing more than the rubber-stamping of something that had taken place long before.

It was different when it opened. A fortnight ahead of the official date of 14 August 1871 to goods, a four-coach special was run to take the lead miners on a seaside outing to Aberystwyth. It joined up at Caersws with a portion that had started from Llanidloes. Later that month another miners' special was

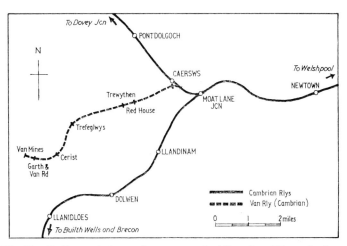

The Van Railway. A short, character-packed line that did not for long remain independent of the Cambrian Railways

run for an important local occasion: the opening of a church at Caersws. Both were isolated workings, as regular passenger services (on which workmen's weekly tickets were two shillings) did not begin until winter 1873. The Van lead mines had been the centre of financial speculation throughout Britain and soon after they changed hands for £42,000, they were rashly valued at more than a million pounds. Sixteen companies employed 700 men for a time until the bubble burst. Mining continued until 1920, and after grouping the GWR found it worthwhile to maintain the line to get high-quality ballast from the spoil heaps of the old mines. The whole story has been well told by Lewis Cozens, a sympathetic chronicler of remote Welsh lines.

The Mawddwy Railway

The Mawddwy Railway added its own distinctive contribution to the individuality of Welsh railways by being different in character from other independent lines that were its neighbours to the west and east—the Van Railway and the Corris Railway. They both served hilly districts while the Mawddwy's duty was to open up the Upper Dovey Valley. The Mawddwy also drew some of its character from the valley and its air of isolation, which the motor age has not removed entirely.

Twelve years after the line opened in 1867, the *Gossiping Guide to Wales* was surprised to find a railway there:

> Now if you were to search Great Britain over, and had to say where would be the most unlikely place to see a railway station, you would say, "At Dinas Mawddwy." And yet there you would find one.

From the Cambrian main line at Cemmes Road, the Mawddwy dropped away amid the fields at the mouth of the valley and then tucked itself on a low embankment (just above flood water level) at the foot of the steeply rising mountains on the west side of the narrowing valley. Its course took it close to slate and silica mines and through the small village of Aberangell. At Dinas Mawddwy the railway did not do so well for it finished up at a terminus half a mile short of the village. A feature that caught the eye of Lewis Cozens was something totally unimportant—an impressive stone gateway at the entrance to the station yard. It was the sort of thing the original company considered more necessary than a shelter for passengers at the exposed station at Mallwyd. Today, the gates are back forming the show-piece entrance to the station (open 1869–1940), which is now used by far more people than ever caught trains from it. The site was taken over in 1966 and developed as a thriving woollen mill. The station waiting room is a cafe, cosily and attractively converted, and other features remain, including the modest goods shed and water column.

Originally the Mawddwy Railway was a one-man concern—that of the Lord of the Manor, Edmund Buckley, who was later knighted. Besides the branch, he built the Hendre-Ddu Tramway as a narrow gauge feeder from a stone quarry at Aberangell. Bradshaw's *Manual* repeatedly summed up the position succinctly: 'No printed accounts issued, the Company being principally the property of the chairman.'

It was not a thriving concern, for the upper Dovey was too small and remote a valley to support a railway, however modest. Passenger services ceased in 1901 and complete closure followed in 1908. But social consciences were awakening and three years later the line was rebuilt and re-opened, this time as a light railway, financially supported by four local councils. The Cambrian ran the system and later the GWR, which withdrew passenger trains, this time for good, in 1931. But freight sustained the Mawddwy for another two decades, so in terms of Forgotten Railways, the Mawddwy is not especially old.

Aberdovey Harbour Branch

It is not the fault of the Cambrian Railways that coast line passengers have their magnificent sea views briefly interrupted by four short tunnels at Aberdovey. When the Aberystwyth &

Welsh Coast line reached the port, its shipping was of tremen-
dous importance—'a harbour equal to Portsmouth', was how
it was described to MPs in 1865. Nothing was to be allowed to
interfere with the ships so the railway had to go round the back
of the houses. And that meant burrowing. But perhaps it need
not have been so, as the trains soon took the wind out of the
sails and Aberdovey's coastal shipping trade was doomed.
However much the shipping and railway interests might have
hated each other, they achieved some sort of harmony and the
Cambrian was duly admitted to the wharves, reached by a
short branch—in effect, a back-shunt for trains arriving from
the south.

Rails ensnared the small quay: two lines went farther out on
to the jetty. Everywhere were turntables for handling single
wagons—the layout was too cramped for anything else. Small
sheds for the export of slates and imports, mainly grain, were
built—and remain. Grain was vital to local people, because for
years there were no phosphates in the soils of Merioneth and
wheat would not grow. In recent years the harbour area has
been developed for Aberdovey's latest form of bread (and
butter), the tourists, who take their evening strolls where trains
once ran, to look at a harbour from which ships once sailed.

For a few brief months, there were Cambrian paddle
steamers, which ran to Waterford after the Company got
authority to operate steamboats in 1889. They soon left Aberdovey because of threats by Euston to make Irish ferry fares
totally uneconomic.

Years earlier (1863–67) passengers and goods were ferried
across the river from Ynyslas on the Aberystwyth line, because
Aberdovey was the southern terminus of an isolated section of
the coast line then being built steadily northwards, Aberdovey
was not connected to the main line until 1867, within a few
weeks of the opening of the entire line to Pwllheli, following
completion of Barmouth bridge. Such little ports once had an
importance of which the holidaymaker of today may never
dream.

The Cambrian's Dolgelley Branch

The $7\frac{1}{4}$ miles of trackbed up the Mawddach estuary from the sand-duned bay at Barmouth Junction (re-named Morfa Mawddach 28 May 1960) to the quieter, mountain-dominated region at Dolgelley (re-named Dolgellau 12 September 1960) is scenically delightful and historically important because of its influence of other lines serving the Cambrian coast. The Cambrian, which built the branch with powers originally obtained by the Aberystwyth & Welsh Coast Railway, used it to defend its vulnerable flank south of Barmouth, as the GWR advanced west from Ruabon, through the Dee Valley and to the coastal gateway at Dolgellau. The main worry was that this would be a much shorter route between the coast and the populous areas of North West England than the Cambrian's roundabout one via Machynlleth. The branch was authorised in 1862 but Penmaenpool (in the middle of glorious nowhere) was the terminus for some years and an end-on junction at Dolgelley was not opened until 1869. The pleasant two-platform station, to which the Cambrian got access via running powers, remained a frontier until the approach of Grouping.

Paddington must have dreamed of having control of the line through to Barmouth Junction and the resort for years, but once it got it, there was work to be done:

> The Engineer has considerable renewal work to do at Dolgelley and a plan has been prepared to improve the existing arrangements at the Barmouth end of the Station, to remodel the Office accommodation, provide a footbridge and additional Cattle Pens. It is under consideration.

That Chester Divisional Report of 1924 also stressed the need for improvements:

> The arrangements at Penmaenpool are antiquated and as the platform requires renewal, the opportunity has been taken of having a plan prepared for a proper crossing loop with an Island platform. This plan is under consideration.

That never happened although the single platform was eventually rebuilt on the Up side of the line, just east of the private road toll bridge across the Mawddach. Penmaenpool is a good place to recapture the branch atmosphere. In 1973 so much remained—the trackbed, the station, a short tunnel and the two-road engine shed. It was the only passing place after improvements, foreshadowed in the Report, were completed in 1927, mainly by strengthening the track and bridges to enable the GWR to use bigger locomotives, notably 43XX Moguls. They dominated passenger traffic almost to closure, with Manors sharing heavier trains in the closing years. Local trains were often in the hands of small tanks and four times on weekdays until 1965 one could catch the locals and enjoy (weather permitting) a journey that the GWR proclaimed as 'one of the most enchanting in the world, giving views of sea, river and mountains'.

GREAT WESTERN RAILWAY.
(CHES' ER DIVISIO.

(For the use of the Company's Servants only).

Signal Department Work,
PENMAENPOOL.

Between the hours of 6-0 a.m. on **Sunday, August 30th**, and 6-0 p.m. on **Thursday, September 3rd**, or until the work is completed, the Signal Department will have occupation at Penmaenpool for bringing into use a new **Signal Box** fixed on the Barmouth end of the Up platform 7 yards on the Dolgelley side of the old signal box; also new signals as follows:—

Form.	Name.	Position.	Distance from Box
	Down Main Distant ...	Up Side of Single line ...	1,301 yds.
	Down Main Home ...	Down Side of Single line ...	363 yds.
	Down Main Inner Home ...	Down Side of Down Main line	26 yds.
2	(1) Down Main Starting ... (2) Down Main to Locomotive Siding Starting ...	Down Side of Single line ...	245 yds.
	Up Main Advanced Starting	Up Side of Single line ...	389 yds.

Penmaenpool re-signalling after Summer season 1936. Some signals survived (in better condition than this notice) closure, for in 1973 they still stood—silently guarding the deserted trackbed

CHAPTER 7

LNWR: in the shadows

Snowdonia

For much of the way between Bangor and Afon Wen, the main road and secondary line kept unobtrusive company and offered princely views of the Menai Strait and Anglesey. But at Caernarvon they separated. Southbound trains called at a pleasant, spacious station on the north-western outskirts and then plunged into a short tunnel under Castle Square, robbing the rail tourist of a close-up view of the Castle. The road did (and does) better, twisting past shops to reach the Square, dominated by walls and turrets. Caernarvon's pageantry is well enough known, but its railway history, while nothing like so colourful or exciting, deserves mention, for the town once had three terminals—an abundance for a place so small, even in Victorian times. It also had a railway which never used any of the terminals.

The Nantlle Railway was the earliest of Caernarvon's railways, incorporated in 1825 as a tramroad to carry slate from quarries in the valley from which it took its name to Caernarvon, the nearest port whence they could be shipped all over the British Isles and to the world. The Nantlle's gauge of 3ft 6in troubled eminent minds. The Stephensons, who were engaged to lay the rails though not to construct the line, felt that it should have been wider—presumably standard gauge.

However, at 3ft 6in the line was successful enough within its isolated context and for some four decades horses plodded its 9¼ miles. Change came only when the Nantlle lay in the path of promoters aiming to link Caernarvon with Cardigan Bay, into

Page 89 Secondary Cambrian. *(Above)* In a year when Europe prepared for another war, a Tanat Valley local of two four-wheel coaches and diminutive 2–4–0T No 1197 awaited departure from Oswestry, June 1938.

(Below) Blodwell Junction in August 1959, with Class 2 2–6–0 46505 running round a ballast train that it had worked from Nantmawr, before setting off for Oswestry.

Page 90 (Above) The rural glory of the Mid Wales Railway in August 1962. Class 2 2–6–0 46511 approaches Llanstephen Halt with the 13.20 Brecon – Moat Lane. Four months later the line closed south of Llanidloes.

(Below) Pantydwr, near the summit of the line (947ft).

which the Cambrian Railways were driving north from Machynlleth. Springboard of the 28-mile link was the Bangor & Carnarvon Railway (*sic*), which had opened in 1852 and established Carnarvon's first terminal. The Carnarvonshire Railway built the line to Afon Wen and in 1867 it opened from there to Carnarvon's second terminal, Pant, which lay on the opposite side of the town centre to the Bangor terminal, which became the main station after the two lines were linked and Pant closed. But that did not happen until 1870, and the year before a branch had opened to serve Llanberis in the heart of Snowdonia. That, too, had its own Caernarvon terminal for a short time.

The Nantlle's route from the south was a good one, and six miles were converted after it was acquired by the Carnarvonshire Railway. One and a half miles eastwards from Penygroes into the jaws of the valley were standardised in 1870 at the insistence of the Board of Trade, although the section beyond Nantlle to the quarries remained at the original gauge and transhipment sidings were built and used for nearly a century more. The section was destined in that time to be the only 3ft 6in gauge track in British Railways' ownership, and one of the few horse-worked lines that BR inherited. Interim ownership was that of Euston, which bought the Carnarvonshire Railway in 1869. Before that it had built just under 12 miles of line, if the conversion of the Nantlle between Penygroes and Carnarvon is discounted. The 12 miles stretched south from Penygroes to Afon Wen. Between there and Portmadoc the Cambrian Railways also had construction powers, and it was that company that built the stretch which is still there today.

Afon Wen (spelt in several ways by railway companies and map makers) was as splendidly situated as Dovey Junction at the southern end of the Cambrian's coast line. It could have hardly been built nearer the sea without being in it! Between Cardigan Bay and Caernarvon there were other junctions, much more sheltered. There was Dinas, exchange point with a narrow gauge line of rather greater substance than the Nantlle

London and North Western Railway.

TOURS THROUGH SNOWDON DISTRICT 1879.

(COMMENCING ABOUT THE MIDDLE OF JUNE)

Arrangements have been made with the Coach Proprietors for a series of Coach Tours through the Snowdon District, in connection with the London and North Western Co.'s trains from Chester, Rhyl, Llandudno, Bangor, Carnarvon, &c. Passengers at the time of starting in the morning are furnished with tickets, which ensure their being provided with seats on the Coaches. The following are particulars of the routes by the various tours.

TOUR No. 1.—By rail to Llanberis, thence by Coach through the "Pass of Llanberis," and past the Swallow Waterfall to Bettwsycoed, and by rail home to the Station from which the Tourist started in the morning.

TOUR No. 2.—By rail to Bettwsycoed, thence through same District as No. 1 Tour to Llanberis. Home by Train.

TOUR No. 3.—By rail to Carnarvon, thence by Coach round Snowdon to Beddgelert, and through the Vale of Gwynant, and the Pass of Llanberis to Carnarvon. Home by Train.

TOUR No. 4.—By rail to Bettwsycoed, thence by Coach past the Swallow Waterfalls, Capel Curig, the Vale of Nant Francon, and the Penrhyn Slate Quarries to Bangor. Home by Train; or Passengers can travel by Train to Bangor, thence by Coach, through the same District, to Bettwsycoed, and home by Train.

TOUR No. 5.—By rail to Llanberis, thence by Coach to Beddgelert, and back to Llanberis. Home by Train.

TOUR No. 6.—By rail to Bettwsycoed, thence by Coach to Beddgelert and back to Bettwsycoed. Home by Tarin.

TOUR No. 7.—By rail to Bettwsycoed, thence by Coach to the Fairy Glen, Conway Falls, Pandy Mill Falls, and along the Pentre Voelas Road as far as Voelas Hall, and back to Bettwsycoed. Home by Train.

TOUR No. 8.—By rail to Llanrwst, thence by Coach to Trefriw and back, and home by Train.

These Routes cover some of the most beautiful scenery in North Wales. Full particulars as to the fares, time of starting, &c., can be obtained from the Special Bills which are issued, and which may be obtained at any of the Principal Stations and Hotels along the North Wales Coast.

CHEAP RETURN TICKETS.

Return Tickets at Cheap Fares are issued from Birmingham, Liverpool, Manchester, Warrington, &c., to the principal places of attraction in North Wales, on Saturdays, available for return on the following Monday.

TOURISTS ARRANGEMENTS.

First, Second, and Third Class Tourist Tickets, available for Two Calender Months, will be issued from May 1st to October 31st inclusive, at the Principal Stations on the London and North-Western Railway, to places of interest and attraction in the United Kingdom.

PIC-NIC AND PLEASURE PARTIES.

From May 1st to October 31st inclusive, First, Second, and Third Class Return Tickets will (with certain limitations) be issued at Reduced Fares to Parties of not less than six first or ten second or third class passengers. Application to be made at any of the Stations at least three days before the date of the proposed excursion.

Any information as to Tourists and Pleasure Party arrangements, Excursion Trains &c., can be obtained on application to Mr. E. Wood, London and North-Western Railway, Chester, Mr. G. P. Neele, Euston Station, London, or to the undersigned

Chief Traffic Manager's Office,   *G. FINDLAY.*
30   *Euston Station, London.*

Euston's praises of North Wales were in print rather than pictures. In Victorian years no one was quite sure when the tourists would start to arrive quarry system: the North Wales Narrow Gauge Railway of 1877, better remembered as the Welsh Highland. It maintained an exchange platform at Dinas, hopeful of the revenue big brother would provide. Also hoping for revenue from the same source was a 'foreigner', the Snowdon Mountain Railway, which maintained the refreshment room at Dinas.

Not all the Nantlle 3ft 6in route was used by the Carnarvonshire Railway: the Tramroad's approach to Caernarvon Harbour was abandoned by the standard gauge builders, who went farther inland. The Caernarvon Town line, linking the Carnarvonshire Railway with the line from Bangor, was built by that company jointly with the Carnarvon & Llanberis Railway; the Bangor & Carnarvon was not involved.

Bangor–Menai Bridge–Caernarvon

There was always something to delight the eye in the short journey between Bangor and Caernarvon. Once clear of Bangor tunnel, there were treetop glimpses of the Menai Strait to Menai Bridge, where a lavish station offered two platforms to both the Holyhead and Afon Wen routes—useful places to get off-beat views of the tubular and suspension bridges. As the sharply-graded Afon Wen line climbed away south, there were notable views of Anglesey, maintained throughout the rest of the journey. It all dated from summer 1852, the time when the Bangor & Carnarvon company, incorporated only the previous year, completed a single line, which was doubled many years later. The first trains were those operated by the Chester & Holyhead company and worked by the LNWR, into which the B & C was swallowed in 1867.

Ultimately Caernarvon offered trains to Bangor or Afon Wen and to Llanberis and its station was more than adequate for those services. But there were times when the little system was strained. The Investiture of the Prince of Wales in summer 1911 was a truly Royal occasion and about 30 specials arrived before half-past ten in the morning. The truncated branch

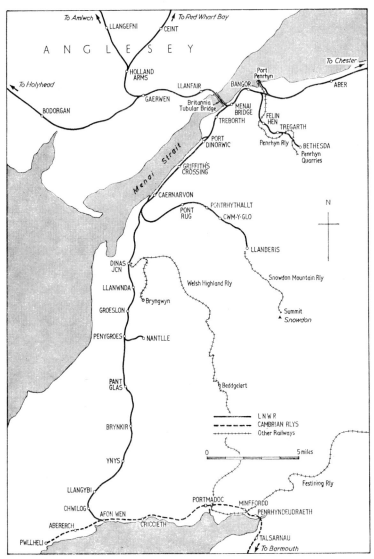

Euston's only rivals around Snowdonia were narrow gauge

survived to see a second Investiture, that of Prince Charles as Prince of Wales in 1969, but then the specials were fewer. That was six years after the Minister of Transport, Mr Ernest (now Lord) Marples, had rejected BR proposals to close the branch. While consenting to closure between Caernarvon and Afon Wen, he retained the Bangor link because Caernarvon was a useful railhead for places further south, including Butlin's Pwllheli camp, which was considered to need a railhead more convenient to North Wales and North West England than could be provided by the Cambrian coast line, with its long feeder route via Machynlleth. The last regular passenger train shuttled between Caernarvon and Bangor on a snowy day in January 1970, but plans for track lifting were soon postponed when the Tubular Bridge caught fire, isolating Holyhead from the rest of BR. Caernarvon became the temporary rail terminal for Irish freight traffic, usually handled at Holyhead. Menai Bridge–Caernarvon finally closed in February 1972.

Port Dinorwic Branch

The only branch off the Bangor & Carnarvon was of just a mile, built probably five years after the parent line opened in 1852. It ran to the attractive, tree-shaded little harbour of Port Dinorwic, beside the sheltered waters of the Menai Strait. It was developed as an outlet for slate from the Dinorwic Quarries near Llanberis, then among the biggest in the world. This reached Port Dinorwic over the Padarn Railway, built to another gauge curiosity, 4ft 0in. Much of the slate was shipped from the Port, but some was transhipped to standard gauge trains at the Harbour sidings—as happened farther north at Port Penrhyn (page 98).

Carnarvon & Llanberis Railway Company

Every approach to Llanberis is impressive: by foot over the mountains; by car through the famous Pass flanking Snowdon, and (until 1964) by rail. The views obtained from the carriage between Caernarvon and Llanberis were perhaps the least rewarding of local panoramas because for much of the way the line was twisting its way up the valley of the river Seiont. Eventually at journey's end (on clear days) came reward, for the passenger stepped on to a single platform dominated by mountains, which provided the backcloth to charming Llyn Padarn.

Close to Seiont and sea at Caernarvon lay the Carnarvon & Llanberis Railway Company's original Pant terminus. Its opening in 1869 marked a milestone in the history of a rather unsuccessful company. A single line authorised to Llanberis in 1864 never materialised because of money shortage, and after four years the company abandoned another line that was to open up a neighbouring valley and its main village Bettws Garmon. Llanberis was only reached after Euston stepped in and provided £50,000 worth of extra capital. The original promoters lacked incentive for they knew there was no chance of winning slate traffic, firmly in the hands of the Padarn Railway.

All was not wasted, and traffic allowed seven local trains a day to and from Llanberis, supplemented by excursions. The local trains were an early LMS casualty, being withdrawn in 1930, but excursions resumed in summer 1932 and weekly goods continued until the branch finally closed.

No attempt was made to re-open the branch (which, in any case, had its legs taken from under it by the Bangor–Carnarvon lifting), but it did figure in ideas considered by enthusiasts anxious to revive the Padarn Railway after that ceased working in October 1961. The most ambitious scheme envisaged a circular route around Llyn Padarn with the branch trackbed on the southern side of the lake linked to that of the Padarn by new track sections at both ends of the lake. Another proposal mooted was to use the Padarn trackbed to Llanrug and then take a line along the track of the Llanberis branch to Caernarvon's outskirts, heading from there, not for the town centre, but south along the Afon Wen branch as far as Dinas and a junction with the revived Welsh Highland Railway. What actually happened was that Caernarvonshire County Council completed in spring 1973 a conversion of the most spectacular section of the LNWR branch into a road to by-pass the congested main street at Llanberis. The by-pass (if you can ignore the traffic) provides a grandstand of lake and mountains. Plans for the Padarn revival settled down into the building of a narrow gauge line (nominally 2ft 0in) along the north shore of the lake. Opened in 1971, just a decade after the Padarn's closure, the Llanberis Lake Railway runs for nearly two miles from Gilfach Ddu at Llanberis to Penllyn, near the opposite end of the lake. So the town retains two railways—the terminal of the Snowdon Mountain Railway being just a short distance from that of the little railway, which keeps to the level.

Bangor–Bethesda

Bangor and Bethesda were first connected by Telford's Holyhead Road, the A5, so it is perhaps not surprising that Euston was not totally successful when it built a short branch (of no more than $4\frac{1}{4}$ miles) to duplicate that reasonable road communication. Incentive was limited, for slate from the quarries that dominated Bethesda (like Llanberis, another of the world's great production districts) was also privately transported to the sea. Euston did not need to be reminded of the fact, as it had three times to get authority to cross the narrow gauge Penrhyn Railway, serving those quarries.

The land Euston used was solely Lord Penrhyn's, and he had regard for the local landscape, insisting that the new branch should be as unobtrusive as possible. The signal box at the junction with the main line was to be built as low as possible; embankments were to be planted with trees and telegraph wires put underground, although this was not to be. Trees, among them one presumes those planted when construction took place, now cover much of the trackbed, and in death as in life, the course of line is well hidden. Buses running along the A5 led to the demise of passenger trains in 1951, but limited freight traffic was able to survive for a dozen more years.

Port Penrhyn Branch

Regret that passenger trains never ran on the 1½-mile branch from Port Penrhyn sidings on the Chester & Holyhead main line a little north of Bethesda Junction, was once expressed by J. M. Dunn, a former shedmaster at Bangor, whose books and articles about North Wales railways have brought pleasure to many enthusiasts. He once pointed out in *The Railway Magazine* that the Port Penrhyn branch ran through some charming scenery that the public had little chance of seeing. Shortly the planners may open up these hidden views; in the Bangor Town Map of 1968 it was proposed that land to the west of and partly adjacent to the trackbed of the branch should become an open space.

The route taken by the branch, opened by the C & H in 1852, ran west of the narrow gauge Penrhyn Railway. It never crossed it, but standard and narrow gauge lines were intertwined on the quay of the little port. Like Port Dinorwic, it was a busy transhipment point, for in the years up to closure of the standard gauge branch in 1963, some 20,000 tons of slate and slate dust were handled in this way, after being brought down from the Penrhyn quarries by the little railway.

Red Wharf Bay

Besides the Chester & Holyhead main line, only two other public lines (the qualification excludes the 7ft 0in gauge Holyhead Harbour Railway between the long breakwater and local quarries, a line since converted to standard gauge and still used) were built in Anglesey. Both were very much branches, rather than secondary routes.

The Anglesey Central Railway was completed between

LMS

WEEKLY RUN-ABOUT TICKETS
·(Go-As-You-Please)
IN
NORTH WALES
ISSUED UNTIL OCTOBER 31st, 1938

AREA No. I		AREA No. 7
Prestatyn Rhyl, Denbigh Ruthin, Abergele Colwyn Bay Llandudno, Llanrwst Bettws-y-Coed Blaenau Festiniog Bangor, Bethesda Caernarvon, Afonwen Amlwch, Holyhead Also Llanberis during the Season	AVAILABLE SEVEN DAYS BY ANY TRAIN	Chester ◆Holywell Town Rhyl, Abergele Denbigh, Mold Ffrith, Corwen Colwyn Bay Llandudno Conway Penmaenmawr Llanfairfechan

ISSUED ANY DAY	THIRD CLASS **10/6** (First Class 15/9)	CHILDREN ·UNDER 14 HALF-FARE (fractions of 1d. as a 1d.)

NOT AVAILABLE BY BUS

FOR MAPS OF AREAS—SEE PAGES 2 & 7

MAP OF NORTH WALES—PAGES 3 to 6

LMS policy was to publicise not only its main routes but to draw attention to branches like Llanberis and Bethesda

Gaerwen and the small port of Amlwch, nearly 19 miles away on the north coast of the island, in 1866. It closed to passengers 7 December 1964 but survives (indeed, thrives) because of the chemical industry that has been established at Amlwch, and in 1974 branch traffic was supplemented when an oil pipeline was laid between a terminal for supertankers constructed off-shore, and Stanlow refinery. In the same year Anglesey County Council began exploring the possibilities of restoring passenger trains. The other branch has been forgotten since 1950. It ran 6¾ miles to Red Wharf Bay from Holland Arms, the first station on the Amlwch branch, 2½ miles north of Gaerwen. Authorised around the turn of the century and completed in 1909, it 'served' rather than reached Red Wharf Bay, for its terminus was half a mile short of the hamlet, and a mile from Benllech, a slightly larger place. Thousands of people go to Red Wharf and its neighbouring bays each summer and enjoy their lovely sands. If the railway had run through to them, they might have developed more as resorts than as centres for caravan and camping sites. Why the railway stopped where it did, remains one of history's mysteries. Closure occurred in two well-spaced stages: to passengers in 1930 and to goods 20 years later. Perhaps the second economy might have come much earlier had there been someone interested in buying the trackbed, for the BR District Estates Surveyor was quoted in the *Liverpool Daily Post* as stating that it took 35 years to sell the branch. This suggests it had been on the market since soon after the end of passenger services.

The Steam of Memory

In the days when Royal Scots and Black Fives and other standard LMS and BR designs were common on the North Wales main line, it was pleasant to go in search of the ageing locomotives, readily found on the branch lines. Around Snowdonia, there were several classes, notably LNWR Coal Tanks and another popular Webb design, the 2–4–2 tanks. The rugged Coal Tanks worked several lines from sheds at Bangor and Caernarvon—a subsidiary shed that handled up to 11 locomotives. They handled one-coach motor-trains to Bethesda, Llanberis and Nantlle.

One of the Coal Tanks, No 1054, has been preserved due to the untiring efforts of J. M. Dunn before his death. After nine years on show at the Industrial Railway Museum at Penrhyn Castle, Bangor, No 1054 was moved in autumn 1973 to its present home at the Dinting Railway Centre near Manchester. The move was made to allow more space at Penrhyn for the display of relics of narrow gauge railways, including the local quarry lines, and other industrial exhibits—a guide is published by the Museum.

The Red Wharf Bay achieved an historical 'first' when it opened, as it was worked by the first LNWR pull-and-push unit, for which two 2–4–0 tanks were converted to the 2–4–2 wheel arrangement. They were the first of that company's locomotives adapted for motor-train working. 'Cauliflower' 0–6–0s also spent retirement years in Snowdonia.

Broadly the intensity of passenger services on the branches was a little heavier than those found on totally rural branches throughout Britain. In 1915 the Bethesda branch was by far the busiest of local lines, handling about a dozen trains each way on weekdays, compared with seven to Nantlle and Llanberis and between Bangor and Afon Wen. The line became tremendously busy after the opening of Butlin's large holiday camp at Penychain, within sight of Afon Wen station. Many of the camp specials (trains of up to 10 coaches from the North West and the Midlands) had to be double-headed south from Bangor, which incidentally, is now advertised as the railhead for the camp, even though the Cambrian coast line remains open. Other holidaymakers travelled over the line on the North Wales Cruise Trains, or on summer locals that ran from Bangor and reversed at Afon Wen to reach Pwllheli. Goods traffic on the branches remained healthy for many years, mainly in the form of local pick-up workings from Bangor, but for many years there was a middle-of-the-night freight to Caernarvon from Mold Junction.

Anyone going in search of Snowdonia's disused lines will soon find that a number of stretches have been comprehensively redeveloped by Caernarvonshire County planners. Notable examples are at Llanberis and Nantlle, where the station yard with its gauge interchange sidings have been altered out of all recognition, although the station building survives as a house.

BR's relinquishment of the Llanberis branch gave planners a golden opportunity to relieve the town's traffic congestion with a by-pass as already mentioned. At Caernarvon, the newly-created Gwynedd County Council, continuing the policy of its predecessor, bought the station site in autumn 1974. It was part of a deal involving 69 acres of land covering 6½ miles of the route to Menai Bridge (between Pont Seiont and a point north of Pont Ty Golchi). The 'land bank' investment cost the authority more than £130,000. It was designed to allow 'urgent' road improvements to be carried out at Port Dinorwic and other places under schemes that will involve the demolition of a number of the old railway bridges.

CHAPTER 8

LNWR: in the Vales

North East Wales

The green fields that form the rolling summit of Hope Mountain, five miles north of Wrexham and yet a world away from its mines and quarries, once provided a grandstand from which to watch the leisurely progress of trains on two pre-grouping routes. Thin plumes of smoke rising from the woods near Hawarden (once Gladstone's home), signalled the approach of

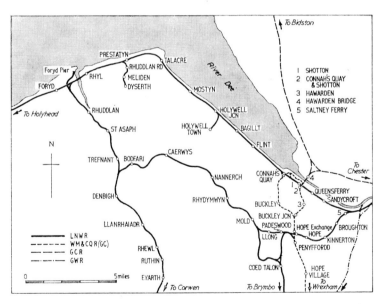

North East Wales, where railways picked their ways without much trouble through the valleys

Wrexham-bound trains from Seacombe or Chester along the WM & CQ line. Their journeys were punctuated by stops at Hope Exchange in the middle distance, where the line passed above that from Chester to Mold and Denbigh, which was the main stem of Euston's system in North East Wales. Although, like the Snowdonian system, it stemmed from the Chester & Holyhead main line, it was different in character.

That was, I think, because the scenery was different. In place of Snowdonia's rugged grandeur, the Clwydian Hills are green and homely, and Euston's aspirations took it through the valleys on both flanks. The North East Wales system had a good pedigree: the Mold Railway, formed in 1847 with powers for a 10-mile line to bring trains from Saltney Ferry, on Chester's western outskirts. The Company was independent until it came to construction, for the Chester & Holyhead paid for most of that; it also worked the Mold Railway from its opening in August 1849 and absorbed it before the end of that year, before it was itself absorbed by the LNWR.

The Mold Railway waited until 1866 to lose its isolation, securing a new, but not very useful, tie with the Wrexham Mold & Connah's Quay through a south-to-west junction and exchange sidings at Penyffordd, supplemented by a two-level exchange platform at Hope Exchange a little to the north. There were plans for improvements at Penyffordd for a spur, south-to-east, to allow trains from Chester to reach Wrexham. Low earthworks are the memorial to that idea of 1880 for rails were never laid.

Hope Exchange survived as a two-level exchange until 1958— a station among fields without road access. I learned that during World War II while returning from a short holiday at Caerwys. The Chester train stopped alright, but the Seacombe connection (four LNER teak coaches and a C13 Atlantic tank), flew past. There was no guarantee that the next train two hours later would not do the same so my parents and I walked to Penyffordd, safety negotiating the Exchange Sidings and spur, where all was peace on a Saturday afternoon in summer.

Today the spur is more useful than it ever has been, as it is used by freight trains anxious to reach Mold, which was something the Wrexham Mold & Connah's Quay never managed. Re-routing over the spur allowed the complete closure, after the end of Chester–Denbigh locals in 1962, of six miles between Hope and Saltney Ferry, including Kinnerton bank, where the Mold Railway climbed away from the flattish plain followed by the Chester & Holyhead, to secure a foothold in the hills. The Penyffordd spur provides access to Mold, also to quarries and industry at Rhydymyn a couple of miles farther north, but the section was little used until a delivery depot for the Anglesey–Stanlow oil pipeline was opened in 1974, when the stretch enjoyed a vigorous renewal of life.

Mold–Denbigh

The stretch to Dolfechlas Crossing is the only surviving piece of the Mold & Denbigh Junction Railway, authorised in 1861 as the natural extension of the Mold Railway. When it opened in 1869 it was able to join the Vale of Clwyd Railway, opened the previous year from Rhyl (Chester & Holyhead main line) to Denbigh. Euston had some bitter rows with the M & DJ about access to Denbigh, quarrels that in good Victorian fashion, lasted for years: ten in this case. Euston, which had the money, insisted that trains from Mold should run direct to Denbigh and not miss it altogether by using a spur, authorised in the Vale of Clwyd Act, which would have allowed them to reach Rhyl and the coast. It was talked about for years, but there was never sufficient spur for a spur. One reason for there being little demand for it was that many of the passengers using the M & DJ were on their way to market at either Mold or Denbigh: no easy days at the seaside for them. Without trains reversing at Rhyl, the route could not have been used as a duplicate to the C & H main line. The M & DJ was partly double-tracked and its trains offered views pastoral rather than dramatic. They reached a summit of 534ft at Star Crossing Halt near Nannerch, which lay at the foot of shapely Moel Arthur, three times that height above sea level.

Vale of Clwyd: Rhyl–Corwen

Cars not only kill the countryside, but people's visions of it as well. Towns, villages, hamlets, wide-views, industrial scenes, sharp bends may be noted during a drive, but memory tends to merge them into one at the end of it. Those going in search of forgotten railways will have to do better. They will have to stop their cars and walk, if only a short distance. Then they will be able to absorb scenes—pretty or industrial—that they will remember. The Vale of Clwyd offers much else to those seeking its old railway—castles and a cathedral and several historic towns, not quite swamped yet by motorists, content to sweep through the lovely vale at the fastest possible speeds en route for either the North Wales seaside or their homes.

Two independent railway companies built the 25 miles between Saltney Ferry and Denbigh. Two more constructed the route some five miles longer from Rhyl to Corwen, and in early days the journey actually involved running for an eye's distance over the metals of two more companies. The Vale of Clwyd Railway, already noted, had no trouble in building 10 miles of single track from Rhyl as far inland as Denbigh. The company was Incorporated in 1856, completed its line in 1858 and made one further addition seven years later, a 1¼-mile branch from a trailing connection at Foryd, on Rhyl's outskirts, to Foryd Pier at the mouth of the Clwyd.

Foryd was the junction for many years of a standard gauge line that meandered through fields for nearly four miles to a big army camp at Kinmel Park near St Asaph. It was constructed during World War I and used for military traffic until 1925 when it became an outlet for nearby St George's quarry. The quarry owners used the line until closure in February 1965.

Page 107 (Above) Dolgellau in 1973 – long after the trains had gone. Platform stones were more accessible to vandals than slates on the roof.

(Below) Travellers reaching Builth Road on the Central Wales line find a transformed scene on the MWR trackbed below.

Page 108 (Above) Tucked away amid the pastoral beauty of the Elan Valley, a contractor's system was used in the construction of the Birmingham reservoirs. An 0–6–0T heads a short train of low-plank wagons. The line crossed Garreg Ddu Viaduct, now a road.

(Below) The Elan Valley never had a public passenger service, but in Snowdonia the summer Bangor – Afon Wen locals often had impressive motive power and corridor stock, as shown in this picture of ex-LMS Class 4 2–6–4T 42585 at Penygroes in August 1961.

Denbigh Ruthin & Corwen

To return to the Vale of Clwyd route, we pick up the metals of the Denbigh Ruthin & Corwen Railway, incorporated in 1860. The railway (though not its builders) paused at Ruthin from 1862 to 1864. Everyone should pause at Ruthin, if only for an hour, to appreciate the splendid hillside setting of the town, never obvious from the train.

By the time the line was extended to Corwen in 1864, that town was being approached from the east by the nearly completed line from Ruabon. The Clwyd builders had been delayed in conquering Eyarth rock cutting with what the *Gossiping Guide* called 'a singular bit of railway engineering'. The railway builders were the third contenders for passage through the wooded gorge, which it had to share with a river and a road. The Guide also claimed that a musician called Mr Hullah was the first passenger they knew who had got out at Ruthin station and failed to find an English porter:

> Indeed one complaint against the Welsh Railway Companies is that so many English servants are employed—to the inconvenience of the native population and the corruption of the Welsh language.

Plenty of Welsh is spoken in Ruthin today, but there are no trains. Euston got total command of the Vale of Clwyd route by absorbing that company in 1868 and its companion 11 years later.

Holywell Town Branch

In 1973 the closed station at Holywell Junction was stated by the National Union of Railwaymen to be the only Victorian station in the whole of Wales that was listed as a preserved building. Most of Holywell's railway history had surrounded the Holywell Town branch, which is worthy of remembrance for several reasons. Not being opened until 1912, it was the last of the branches to stem from the Chester & Holyhead. It ran up a narrow valley on a steady gradient of 1 in 27 which made it one of the steepest lines in Britain worked by ordinary locomotives, in later years invariably a Webb Coal tank with a one-coach motor train on which the locomotive was always at the main line end. The only halt, St Winefride's, lay some distance from the famous Well.

The prosperous, narrow valley was packed with diverse industry: lead mining and copper smelting being carried on beside flannel and paper making. In the middle of the last century a 3ft 0in gauge tramway was built to carry lead and limestone mined in the hills above the town to the harbour on the river Dee at Greenfield and for a time it was reputed to have crossed the C & H on the level. The need for something better

MOLD, COED TALON, AND BRYMBO. Week days only. One class only.

(timetable for Mold, Coed Talon, and Brymbo — columns of departure and arrival times, including "Week days only", "Saturdays only", "Weds. & Sats. only" designations)

HOLYWELL JUNCTION AND HOLYWELL TOWN. Week days only. One class only.

(timetable for Holywell Junction, St Winefride's, Holywell Town — columns of departure and arrival times)

PRESTATYN AND DYSERTH. Week days only. One class only.

(timetable for Rhyl, Prestatyn, Chapel Street, Rhuddlan Road, Meliden, Dyserth — columns of times, including "Mondays only", "Saturdays only", "Saturdays only")

RHYL, ST. ASAPH, AND DENBIGH. Week days only.

(timetable for Rhyl, Rhuddlan, St Asaph, Trefnant, Denbigh — columns of times, including "One class" designations)

Goodbye to all That—Robert Graves' classical story of life in the trenches was written, among other years, in 1915. And so it has proved to be with many of the branches listed in the LNWR Time Tables from 1 October 1915, although Dyserth is still open for quarry traffic than a tramway led to the formation in 1864 of the Holywell Railway Company to build a line of standard gauge between the town and harbour, and to connect with the LNWR, with which the company made a working agreement. However, the scheme was abandoned after only four years.

The branch of 1912 was one for which the LNWR itself had obtained authority six years earlier. Euston's publicity experts seem to have forgotten the line, for several years after it opened the company still noted the line between Atherton and Bolton (Great Moor Street) as the most steeply-graded over which it ran passenger trains. Shortly before the Holywell branch opened, the LNWR experimented with road motors in the area, presumably to test their hill-climbing capabilities. Closure of the branch to passengers in 1954 was no surprise, nor the demise, three years later, of the quarter-mile stub that had continued to provide rail access to local textile mills.

Ffrith Branch

Another line along which freight trains had to struggle was the Ffrith branch, of pure Chester & Holyhead vintage. It stemmed from the Mold Railway and ran four miles to Llanfynydd where there were quarries, but it got most of its traffic from a substantial private system which ran from Coed Talon, one of the intermediate villages, to coal mines around the small village of Nerquis.

Nerquis Railway

About the time that the Ffrith branch was ready, the private system which came to be known as the Nerquis Railway was running nine trains a day to dispatch coal from the pits. By the 1860s the system was putting so much coal on to the LNWR that Euston's financial experts sat up and took an interest. A take-over offer met no opposition and in 1866 Euston got Parliamentary authority to do so, to reconstruct and re-align the system and extend it northwards to another junction with the old Mold Railway, just south of that town. Ownership was transferred in 1868 and extension completed two years later. The line now stretched nearly four miles north from Coed Talon and it ran through a deep valley, wide enough for much of the way for only a single track.

Passenger trains used it for years as part of their route between Mold and Brymbo. This formed part of two routes which until 1930 people *could* use to travel between Wrexham and Mold. Both demanded changes of trains. From Wrexham Central one could travel over the WM & CQ to Hope Exchange, or from Wrexham General little chocolate-and-cream trains would take one up the valley and past the steelworks to Brymbo.

Wrexham & Minera Extension Railway

The next stage of the journey would be over the Wrexham & Minera Extension Railway, mentioned briefly among Wrexham's railways in Chapter 2. It was the last line to reach Brymbo, closing a three-mile gap from Llanfynydd on the Ffrith branch.

My idea of a short 'get away from it all' route was for years conditioned by thoughts of the last line to reach Brymbo. Trains ran almost the entire way from Mold through valleys, green and deep, with hardly (in the closing years at any rate) a hint of industry.

The GWR Brymbo branch of 1862 was known as the Wrexham & Minera Railway, since it incorporated the original, least hilly section of the first branch north of Broughton. The Wrexham & Minera Extension Joint Railway was authorised in 1865 and leased in the following year to the GWR and LNWR. It was not until 1872 that it arrived at Brymbo from the north.

For so short a line (it failed by 300yd to reach three miles), the attention that the W & ME enjoyed from the big companies was lavish. The line was built and jointly worked and owned by LNWR and GWR which reaped useful rewards, for it was well endowed with industrial sidings, the staple fabric of the minor branches in Victorian times. After Grouping the LMS provided locomotives and men for all workings, but Paddington liked to display a show of strength now and then, the Chester Division reporting in 1924:

> The Great Western Company occasionally run a goods train from Croes Newydd on to the Branch in the early morning, it being more economical to work it from that end. The mileage is equated.

And so it was—on distances from the GWR milepost at Brymbo —32¾ miles from Shrewsbury; 15¾ from Chester.

The gem hereabouts was Coed Talon, but its triangular junction, where the Ffrith branch made a two-prong meeting with the Mold–Brymbo lines, was not eternal. A cheerful pub remains alongside the site of the little station, never more than a modest single platform with brick buildings. There was plenty of interest—a small wagon works (again, brick; there was nothing temporary about the structure), on the opposite side of the track; a small yard, which handled traffic from several collieries; two small oil works; a quarry (fed by incline) and a brick and tile works. All but the wagon works (now a private house), have been bulldozed and the land partly re-developed. A visitor trying to visualise it all (even using a 6in map) gets little help from the surroundings.

All the former LNWR lines in North East Wales have the merit of lying close to main roads likely to be used by anyone touring or heading for the coast between Llandudno and Prestatyn. All the remains are easily accessible. Gradually the trackbeds are being developed: road improvements are a good guide to the presence of an old line, while confirmation is quickly found among grassy tracks guarded by long and straight hedges.

Train Services

What sort of locomotives and trains does one etch on to the

canvas of one's memory? The lines centred on Denbigh were of two distinct kinds. That to Chester was an important secondary line, heavily freight-laden at the Chester end during World War II. The Vale of Clwyd route was very much a branch. A small shed just north of Denbigh station was the home of several Webb 2–4–2 tanks up to the end of LMS days, and several of those locomotives had carried their LNWR numbers for at least three years after Grouping. Crewe Works paid them scant attention. Later, Chester passenger services were generally in charge of 4–4–0s—the last of the King George V and Precursor classes (allocated to Chester) taking turns with LMS Class 2 4–4–0s and Compounds. Then came LMS and BR 2–6–4 tanks together with LMS standard class 6400 Moguls. Pick-up freights were the duty of standard LMS 0–6–0s, but heavier trains between Rhydymwyn and Chester were sometimes handled by LMS standard 2–8–0s: I once saw one, looking lonely with only a brake van, at Caerwys.

The passenger service was good when one considers the number of trains relative to the number of fields! In 1915 Denbigh had eight trains each way to Chester and they offered London connections. Five were extended to and from Corwen. There were also several locals serving Ruthin. Corwen–Chester took a leisurely two hours, a schedule that allowed for the occasional bit of station working which the discerning eye might spot on a branch line; two five-gallon cans which went into the guard's van at Mold carried the daily water supply for the station and house at Llong.

Rhyl and Denbigh did well for rail communication, being linked by a dozen trains each way, though the half hour allowed for 11 miles was rather more than a motorist allows for the road journey today.

In the Vale of Clwyd, the end of passenger services did not mean the end of passenger trains, for the North Wales Land Cruises jogged along with their merry holidaymakers for a decade. Webb tanks had charge for years of the Mold–Brymbo trains, which stabled in a special siding at Brymbo. The normal daily four trains were supplemented by a late evening one (though well before closing times) twice weekly.

To Remember

These and so many other trains added something to the Welsh scene, yet they were taken for granted as buses are today. Occasionally in summer one will still find steam, though it is unpleasant for it comes from cars with engines overheating in traffic jams! At such times it is perhaps permissible to dream of the days of steam, which weren't so bad after all, and of the railways of Wales—all Wales—so distinctive in character; and the hills and mountains of the glorious backcloth that nature provided for them.

NORTH WALES
RADIO LAND CRUISE

A Circular RAIL Tour
through some of Britain's finest scenery.
FOR MAP OF ROUTE — SEE BACK PAGE.

TUESDAYS AND THURSDAYS
7th July to 23rd July, 1959 (inclusive)
ALSO

MONDAYS TO FRIDAYS
27th July to 4th September, 1959
(INCLUSIVE)

A commentator will supply information on the principal features of interest, and popular music or B.B.C. radio programmes—news items, etc. will be provided at suitable intervals during the cruise.

These brief notes are offered to passengers to assist in following the route taken and to provide a record of what is acknowledged to be a most attractive tour. All references are given facing the direction of travel.

PWLLHELI TO BARMOUTH

Within a few minutes of leaving PWLLHELI we pick up passengers at Penychain, the station serving Butlin's Holiday Camp which is situated on each side of the railway. We then pass through Afon Wen, the junction for the London Midland Region North Wales coast line, over part of which the return journey is made. Criccieth is next reached, a pleasant little watering place of some antiquity with the castle, rebuilt by Edward I in 1285, perched upon a green hill projecting from the sea-front. Conspicuous on a hill behind the town is the residence of the late Earl David Lloyd George.

The route then runs inland to Moel-y-gest and on to Portmadoc which in earlier days was the shipping port for the slate industry of Ffestiniog. From Portmadoc we cross the Glaslyn, leave the county of Caernarvonshire behind and enter Merionethshire where the mountainous range of Snowdonia comes into sight. Here may be obtained a superb view of Y Wyddfa, the central peak of Snowdon at the head of the valley beyond Beddgelert. After traversing the embankment across the mouth of the reclaimed Traeth Mawr and passing through the scattered quarrying villages of Minffordd and Penrhyndeudraeth we reach the beautiful estuary known as Traeth Bach. On through Talsarnau we skirt the flat expanse of Morfa Harlech, with (on our left) an approaching view of Harlech castle rising some 200 feet above the level marshes, on a huge crag platform in a noble situation and conspicuous for many miles. It is a singularly complete and well preserved example of the Edwardian system of concentric fortification.

Proceeding through Llanbedr and Pensarn we pass over the broad marsh of Morfa Dyffryn which extends to the sea on our right, while further on our left are Rhinog Fawr (2,362 feet) and Rhinog Fach (2,333 feet). Next comes Dyffryn Ardudwy station with the comparatively dull western slopes of the Llawellch

BRITISH RAILWAYS

Gazetteer

One day, I suppose, people will go on holiday in Wales in winter and find a haunting loneliness and beauty that summer crowds destroy. Sportsmen go out in all weathers—so, too, should enthusiasts searching old railways. After all, they were operated in all weathers and there is nothing like a winter downpour (and the mist that accompanies it) to wash quickly from the mind excess sentiment and regret about something that has gone!

The surviving Chester & Holyhead main line, the Conway Valley branch and the lines to Wrexham (Chapter 1) offer good introductions to Wales and the Border Country.

Map references have been omitted in instances where remains or places can be found easily without them. Relics mentioned are those likely to be with us for some time to come.

Abbreviations indicate:

Act: Date of Act of Parliament

Remains: Surviving features of note.

Uses: Purposes to which railway buildings and land have been adapted.

Pass: Passenger traffic: date of opening or withdrawal.

Gds: Goods traffic: date of opening or withdrawal.

An asterisk distinguishes lines and places of especial merit. Closure dates of individual stations are given only if the economy was made before passenger services were withdrawn over an entire route.

CHAPTER 2: WREXHAM

Wrexham is now much more important as a road centre than as one of railways, but its shrunken system of lines still seems just a little different from many places. Lower-quadrant GWR signals and trains that never run fast (they are either station stopping or negotiating speed-restricted junctions), and broadly non-modernised stations, help Wrexham to retain something of its atmosphere of earlier years. Of its existing lines, the Shrewsbury & Chester is by far the oldest, forming part of the section opened from Chester (Saltney Junction, with running powers to Chester station) to Ruabon on 4 November 1846. To that was grafted the Brymbo branch from Croes Newydd on 22 May 1862. The Wrexham Mold & Connah's Quay (now used by dmu's to Birkenhead North) was completed to Buckley on 1 May 1866.

Wrexham's two locomotive sheds, always fascinating because of the variety they housed, have been demolished. The former WM & CQ (Great Central) shed at Rhos Ddu (84K) closed on 4 January 1960 and a Remploy factory has been built on the site. The former GWR shed at Croes Newydd (84J) closed in March 1967 and was demolished in 1974/5, although sidings were retained for diesel stabling. Croes Newydd was the parent depot for Bala, Penmaenpool & Trawsfynydd.

RHOS ROBIN (WHEATSHEAF JUNCTION)–MINERA   6 miles
North Wales Mineral Railway

Search demands a foot-slog, and not an easy one at that. The railway was forced across the lie of the hilly land; nothing was allowed to get in the way of the shortest route from the NWMR main line between Chester and Wrexham and local pits and quarries. Only between Wheatsheaf Junction and Gwersyllt does a road parallel the trackbed; elsewhere roads follow contours and so take more practical routes.

ACTS: 1845. North Wales Mineral Railway (Incorporated 6 August 1844) amalgamated with Shrewsbury, Chester & Oswestry 30 June 1845 and formed Shrewsbury & Chester 28 August 1846. Became part of GWR 1 September 1854.
OPENED: July 1847 (*Gds* only); Brymbo–Coed Poeth: 15 November 1897 (*Pass*); Coed Poeth–Berwig: June 1905 (*Pass*).
CLOSED: 22 May 1862: Moss–Brymbo (Brake Incline abandoned on opening of GWR Brymbo branch from Croes Newydd); October 1908: Gwersyllt–Moss (½ mile including lower of two original inclines); 1 January 1931: Withdrawal of Wrexham General–Brymbo–Berwig passenger service; 1951: Wheatsheaf Junction–Gwersyllt (*Gds*); 1 January 1972: Brymbo West Junction–Minera (*Gds*).
REMAINS: *Brymbo–Minera*: trackbed easy to trace; *Brymbo*: tunnel mouth of NWMR branch hidden in cliffside by thick trees: houses on ridge above (301535): *Moss*: widening near road bridge at in-

cline top (south side)—site of small locomotive shed. Trackbed in line with Brake Methodist Chapel: incline descended immediately east (305535); *Gwersyllt*: bridge abutment beside Wheatsheaf Inn on A541 (318532). Trackbed to Wheatsheaf Junction identifiable by double line of overhead power cables on poles.

USES: *Minera–Brymbo*: trackbed offered by British Rail to Wrexham Rural District Council in 1973 for £200, though one councillor was sceptical of value. He warned that the council would have to take over covenants to maintain culverts and fences, which would be liabilities. In the same year, the owners of Minera quarries, which have the second largest limestone output in North Wales, suggested converting the trackbed from Coedpoeth into a road to give better quarry access. *Moss Valley*: trackbed obliterated in landscaping of large area lying between the two inclines. *Summerhill*: rope-worked lower incline adapted as grassy, tree-overhung pathway: a 'breather' between post-war housing estates (315534). *Rhosrobin*: demolition of road overbridge on B5425 planned 1975 (329529).

BRYMBO–LLANFYNYDD (Wrexham & Minera Joint Extension Railway)—see Gazetteer, Chapter 8.

WREXHAM (CROES NEWYDD)–BROUGHTON   3 miles
Great Western Railway

As typical an ex-GWR industrial branch as any that survive, both in surroundings and character. To call it a 'new' GWR Brymbo branch would be misleading for at Broughton the line joined one of the original NWMR branches, which ran down the valley from Brymbo en route to Southsea Colliery. Coal originally reached the Shrewsbury & Chester at Wheatsheaf Junction after being reversed at Brymbo and worked down the inclines.

ACT: 17 May 1861. Joint Lease to LNWR & GWR (Act: 11 June 1866). Vested in GWR 31 July 1871.
OPENED: 22 May 1862 (Gds); 1866 passenger service begun, but discontinued after an unknown period. Resumed 24 May 1882.
CLOSED: 1 January 1931 (Pass). Line remains open to serve Brymbo Steelworks, via shunt-back from Brymbo Middle over GWR Vron branch. Brymbo branch singled for short distance near Croes Newydd to run under Wrexham by-pass, opened 1974.
REMAINS: Original NWMR Southsea branch, closed beyond

Broughton, can be discerned on south-west side of slag heaps of collieries served by the branch: Southsea (closed 1938), Broughton (closed 1878) and New Broughton (closed 1910). The branch was crossed on the level by WMCQ and new connection just south of it was put in at New Broughton (Plas Power) 30 November 1954.

VRON BRANCH 1¼ miles
Brymbo Middle–Vron Colliery
North Wales Mineral Railway
ACT: 1845.
OPENED: November 1847.
CLOSED: The line was shortened by about ¼ mile when Vron colliery closed in 1930, but the rest provides access to steelworks. One can watch steel and coke trains shunt back from Brymbo to the works, but inside, it is private.

WREXHAM (BRYMBO JUNCTION)–BRYMBO (WM & CQ) 4¼ miles
Wrexham Mold & Connah's Quay

The GWR had the best route to Brymbo, but the WM & CQ got a good bonus from its more roundabout one, for it served collieries in competition with Paddington. But geography was against the smaller company when it came to passenger traffic for this line ran only through fields.

ACT: 18 August 1882.
OPENED: Brymbo Junction–Moss & Pentre: 1882 (*Gds*); Moss & Pentre–Plas Power: 1884 (*Gds*); Plas Power–Brymbo: December 1887 (*Gds*). Whole route: 1 August 1889 (*Pass*).
CLOSED: 1 March 1917 (*Pass*); 5 October 1970 (*Gds*). In between —connection near Plas Power (WM & CQ) to GWR Brymbo branch opened 30 November 1954 and Plas Power–Gatewen closed. (Lifted 1958.) New connection—Brymbo GC and Vron re-opened to goods same date. Closed again 19 June 1958 and re-opened second time 1 March 1965. *Gatewen*: 14 March 1960 (*Gds*).
REMAINS: *Gwersyllt*: derelict bridge over Wrexham–Mold road, A541 (320525); *Broughton*: overgrown platform edges of Moss & Pentre station (312518).
SETTING: Like the GWR Brymbo branch, this proved to be another exercise in how to take a railway through a basically populated area away from villages—visit Moss if you challenge that thought! No one can have been sorry when Brymbo station was

well and truly buried under a man-made cliff on which the steel-works have been extended. Few stations could have been more depressing for passengers for it was dominated (almost totally overwhelmed) by the steelworks, high above.

USES: Trackbed near New Broughton has been converted into a road for lorries carrying coal from opencast sites to the rail delivery depot on the site of Gatewen Colliery (312518).

BRYMBO–VRON COLLIERY   ¾ mile
Wrexham Mold & Connah's Quay

Like the GWR, the WM & CQ had to suffer a shunt-back to reach Vron Colliery, the valley slopes being too steep for a direct, frontal attack. WM & CQ branch began from a much lower level but climbed to the colliery without too much difficulty.

ACT: 18 August 1882.
OPENED: 8 October 1888.
CLOSED: 5 October 1970.
REMAINS: Traces of trackbed (298532). *Vron*: branch joins GWR just before colliery and junction can be made out.

WREXHAM (MOSS VALLEY JUNCTION)–MOSS   3 miles
Great Western Railway

OPENED: 11 May 1882 (*Gds*); 1 May 1905 (*Pass*).
CLOSED: Wrexham–Moss local service 1 January 1931 (*Pass*); 1935 (*Gds*).
USES: Track relaid from Moss Valley Junction past site of Gatewen Halt to immediately south of Pentre Broughton Halt (311522) to provide access to Gatewen rail delivery depot.

MOSS–FFRWD   1¼ miles
North Wales Mineral Railway

ACT: 1846.
OPENED: November 1847 (*Gds* only).
CLOSED: Westminster Colliery–Ffos-y-go: 1917; Moss–Westminster Colliery: 1925.
USES: Trackbed obliterated by recent landscaping of the valley.

Moss–Brynmally   ½ mile
North Wales Mineral Railway
ACT: 1846.
OPENED: November 1847 (*Gds* only).
CLOSED: 1935.
USES: Trackbed absorbed in landscaping.

Ffrwd Junction–Local Collieries
Wrexham Mold & Connah's Quay
ACT: 7 August 1862.
OPENED: 1 January 1866 (minerals only).
CLOSED: 1935. First ½-mile retained as shunting neck to sidings
   beside WM & CQ main line.
REMAINS: *Windy Hill* (306549): minor road bridge with twin arches
   for WM & CQ branch (west) to Ffos-y-go Colliery and colliery's
   own line. Trackbed beneath now a woodland glade. *Gwersyllt*:
   trackbed (heavily overgrown), can be traced for about 50yd
   where it climbed away from main line (313551).

Buckley–Connah's Quay   5 miles
Buckley Railway

    The Buckley Railway must have been one of the most intensely
(and economically) worked single lines in Wales, for brickworks and
quarries were strung along it like tightly-packed beads. In the main,
it replaced a quite extensive yet primitive system of tramways. Not
being standard gauge these tramways are outside the scope of this
book but relics of them are on show in the Hawkesbury outdoor
museum at Buckley: see *Country Quest* Magazine for Wales, the
Border & Midlands, September 1974.

ACTS: Authorised 14 June 1860. Buckley Railway leased to WM &
   CQ for 999 years from 30 June 1873. Absorbed by Great Central
   Railway 1 January 1905. Grouped into LNER 1 January 1923.
OPENED: 7 June 1862 (*Gds*). No regular passenger service.
CLOSED: 1959 northern section: Northop Hall Colliery–Connah's
   Quay; 5 July 1965 Northop Hall–Buckley.
REMAINS: *Northop Hall*: bridge abutments in dip on A55 Chester–
   North Wales coast road (273674); *Connah's Quay*: low bridge
   (barred to all but the smallest locomotives) under A548 Chester–
   North Wales coast road, which follows the Dee estuary (293698);
   within sight of derelict station building, which mainly served

Chester & Holyhead main line, but had a branch platform.
Sidings lay between station and main road. Also extant: trackbed
and bridge under C & H main line near river quay.

USES: Northop Hall: trackbed adapted as small coal yard (275679);
garden of private house extended across trackbed and level-
crossing gate restored and incorporated into drive (276668).
Connah's Quay: demolition of bridge across secondary road
(B5126) allowed elimination of sharp, S-bend (tricky to negotiate
when cycling downhill!) (290689); trackbed obliterated by
parkland fringing new housing estate (293696).

BUCKLEY JUNCTION–BUCKLEY   Almost 1 mile
Wrexham Mold & Connah's Quay
ACT: 7 August 1862 (WM & CQ Act of Incorporation).
OPENED: 1 January 1866 *(Gds)*; 1 May 1866 *(Pass)*.
CLOSED: February 1895 *(Pass)*; 3 May 1965 *(Gds)*.
REMAINS: Buckley: station yard heavily overgrown and also ex-
change sidings with brickwork tramways (290645).
USES: Trackbed converted into public footpath; *Buckley Junction* (re-
named Buckley 6 May 1974); station buildings converted and
extended to form small factory. Still a halt for Wrexham–
Birkenhead dmu's.

CONNAH'S QUAY–SHOTTON (HAWARDEN BRIDGE
JUNCTION)   1 mile
Wrexham Mold & Connah's Quay
ACT: 29 June 1883 (with WM & CQ Hawarden Loop Line:
Buckley–Shotton direct).
OPENED: 31 March 1890 *(Gds* only).
CLOSED: 4 September 1967 (traffic ceased from 1 April).
USES: Trackbed on low embankment close to river Dee, opposite
Shotton Steelworks, adapted in places as footpath as part of park
lying alongside C & H main line just north of Shotton (Low
Level, re-opened 17 August 1972). (Park: 305682.) *Connah's
Quay:* trackbed at approach to wharves used for small industrial
estate.

CHAPTER 3: RUABON DISTRICT

Ruabon's sole-surviving railway is the Shrewsbury & Chester,
opened on 4 November 1846 from Chester (Saltney Junction, with
running powers into Chester station) to Ruabon, which remained

the passenger terminus until the line was completed south to Shrewsbury on 14 October 1848. It includes notable viaducts over the Dee, still worth seeing, near the Pontcysyllte canal aqueduct, which gets all the praise, and across the Ceiriog valley at Chirk. For details of closure of Llangollen line Junction, Ruabon, see Chapter 4. Two landmarks of Ruabon's decline have been the closure to goods traffic from 12 January 1964, and reduction to an unstaffed halt (with Chirk) from 1 April 1974. A local man applied in January 1975 to use the empty station buildings for recycling waste computer paper.

RUABON–LEGACY (PONKEY BRANCH)   3 miles
Great Western Railway

Associate of the Rhos branch, very similar in character.

ACT: None. Constructed under 1873 agreement with Henry Dennis, Wrexham colliery owner.

OPENED: 1 August 1861: Ruabon–Aberderfyn (*Gds*); 27 August 1876: Aberderfyn–Legacy (*Gds*), 5 June 1905 (*Pass*). No passenger service over rest of branch, Ruabon–Aberderfyn.

CLOSED: 22 March 1915: Ruabon–Legacy (*Pass*); 1917: Aberderfyn–Legacy (*Gds*); short length at Legacy retained as siding; 25 October 1954: Ruabon Brick & Terra Cotta Company–Aberderfyn (*Gds*); 31 August 1964: Ruabon (Gardden Lodge Junction)–Ruabon Brick & Terra Cotta Company.

REMAINS: Embankment alongside A483, Ruabon (305445). Rest of line now mainly developed.

TREVOR–RHOS (RUABON BROOK TRAMWAY)   3¾ miles
Great Western Railway

One of the more substantial and historic of Ruabon's industrial lines, which kept local traffic between pit and factory off the S & C main line.

ACT: 1794: Ellesmere Canal Company, 1846: Company became Shropshire Union Railways & Canal Company. 1847: Leased to LNWR 12 February 1896: Acquired by GWR (except for lines around Pontcysyllte Canal basin).

OPENED: 26 November 1805: Pontcysyllte—Acrefair (*Gds*); 1808: Acrefair–Plas Madoc Colliery. After 1808: Acrefair–Wynn Hall Colliery: 1860 onwards: tramway converted to railway and opened to Rhos 30 January 1867 (*Gds* only). Wynn Hall Halt–Rhos had railmotor service 1 March 1905–22 March 1915.

Page 125 Snowdonia interchanges. *(Above)* Dinas, about 1911, showing North Wales Narrow Gauge (later Welsh Highland Railway) yard and interchange sidings on the right. A LNWR 'Cauliflower' 0–6–0 Works. Bangor – Afon Wen local.

(Below) Nantlle in 1961. The 3ft 6in tramway tracks in the foreground ran to local slate quarries. The station platform was served by standard gauge, which can just be discerned. The station still survived in 1974.

Page 126 (Above) Red Wharf Bay & Benllech in 1949, one of two 'flattish' branches in Anglesey. Its parent, from Holland Arms to Amlwch, is a freight 'boom' line.

(Below) Holywell Town was at the head of one of the steepest standard gauge lines in North Wales, a bank mainly at 1 in 27. Even the station platform was on a grade of 1 in 50.

CLOSED: Pontcysyllte–Pant: 1953 (completely); Pant–Rhos: 14 October 1963 (completely); Trevor Goods–Pontcysyllte (Monsanto Chemical Works): 1 January 1968.

REMAINS: *Trevor*: cleared station yard lies on south side of Ruabon–Llangollen road (A539). *Acrefair*: traces of level crossing on minor road which formed part of the privately-owned section of the Trevor–Rhos line (274427). *Pontcysyllte*: basin served by railway overgrown since track was lifted; warehouse where locomotives took water has been demolished. Bridge carrying minor road over canal basin entrance also includes arch under which trains shunted to reach canal (272424). Nearby is a stone railway embankment braced by old rails.

USES: *Acrefair*: Low Level goods shed in private use (279429).

RHOS–WREXHAM (RHOS JUNCTION) 3¼ miles
Great Western Railway

The Rhos branch was the GWR's means of serving several quite large, fully-choral Welsh pit and brick villages lying a little west of the Shrewsbury & Chester. In the end, buses ran through village streets to Wrexham's shops while the railway, because its builders could take it nowhere else, ran mainly through the fields. But the coal and the newly-made bricks which even this short branch could collect was sufficient to keep the signal box at Rhos Junction open for sixteen hours a day for many years. Scrappy, insubstantial remains come to life when one remembers the line's value.

ACT: 20 July 1896.
OPENED: 1 October 1901 (*Gds*); 1 March 1905 (*Pass*).
CLOSED: 1 January 1931 (*Pass* excursions until mid 1950s); 14 October 1963 (*Gds*).
REMAINS: *Rhos*: overgrown platform; *Talwrn*: trackbed (295483).
USES: *Rhostyllen*: trackbed cleared for Wrexham by-pass, opened 1974 (309487).

RUABON–PLAS MADOC–DELPH (PLAS MADOC BRANCH) 1¼ miles
Great Western Railway

ACT: Built under Ellesmere Canal Act 1794 (as Ruabon Brook tramroad).
OPENED: 1829: as tramroad, c1867: converted to railway, partly on new alignment. Worked by New British Iron Company until 1886, then Wynnstay Colliery Company. 12 February 1896: sold to GWR.

CLOSED: 1927: Ruabon (*Wynnstay Colliery*)–Plas Madoc. Also short branch to Acrefair. 1953: Plas Madoc–Delph.

REMAINS: First 200yd from junction with main line to local road can still be traced. *Plas Madoc*: short tunnel under A539 by crossroads to Rhos and A483 to Oswestry (290436); overbridge near 'Cheshire Farm' carried branch from Plas Madoc branch to New British Colliery (283435).

USES: *Plas Madoc*: railway and industrial land swallowed by housing estate.

WHITEHURST–FRON   ¾ mile
Great Western Railway

More a long siding than a branch. Ran along wooded hillside.

ACT: None. Worked by Shrewsbury & Chester and later GWR under agreement of 4 March 1845 'as though it is a part of the S & C main line'. Agreement ahead of formation of S & C on 30 June 1845. Finally, the branch was an intermediate siding under control of station master at Whitehurst Halt (287401).

CLOSED: 1930s.

REMAINS: Trackbed has disappeared under thick growth on embankment of Shropshire Union Canal at southern approach to Pontcysyllte Aqueduct. Dip in earthworks beside main line just north of overbridge carrying A5 above the line, marks junction of Fron branch.

USES: Plans for a country park and leisure pursuits centre at Froncysyllte, announced in 1974, including converted limekilns (served by the Fron branch) into a museum.

CHAPTER 4: GWR SECONDARY

RUABON–DOLGELLEY   44½ miles
Great Western Railway

Merioneth County Council and other local authorities bought the trackbed of most of the line from BR after closure. That is among the reasons why holidaymakers can enjoy steam, narrow-gauged and gentle. It marks the progress of summer trains that rattle along the Bala Lake Railway, progressively advancing towards the town from its headquarters at the opposite end of the Lake at Llanuwchllyn (880300)*, where the two-platform station with signal box now sees more passengers than ever it did.

ACTS: 1 August 1859: Vale of Llangollen Railway (Ruabon–Llangollen); 6 August 1860: Llangollen & Corwen Railway; 30 June 1862: Corwen & Bala Railway; Bala & Dolgelly [*sic*] Railway. August 1877 B & D absorbed by GWR; 1 July 1896: other three companies absorbed by GWR.

OPENED: Ruabon–Llangollen 1 December 1861 (*Gds*), 2 June 1862 (*Pass*); Llangollen–Corwen 1 May 1865 (*Pass* and *Gds*); Corwen–Llandrillo 16 July 1866; Llandrillo–Bala Old (later Bala Lake Halt), 1 April 1868; Bala Old–Dolgelley: 4 August 1868. Opening dates of Halts: Sun Bank 24 July 1905; Bonwm 21 September 1935; Llangower 10 June 1929; Llys 4 June 1934; Garneddwen 9 July 1928; Wnion 5 June 1933; Dolserau 8 February 1935.

CLOSURE: 13 December 1964: Llangollen (Goods Junction)–Bala Junction (*Pass* and *Gds*). Ahead of scheduled closure to all traffic of Llangollen (Goods Junction)–Dolgelley on 18 January 1965 because floods cut line at Llandderfel. 18 January 1965: Ruabon–Llangollen (*Pass*); Bala–Bala Junction–Dolgelley (*Pass* and *Gds*). 1 April 1968 Ruabon–Llangollen (Goods Junction) (*Gds*). Closure dates of Halts: Sun Bank 5 June 1950; Garneddwen 4 November 1963; Dolserau 29 October 1951.

REMAINS: Trackbed easily traced along entire route. *Ruabon*: South Junction: Trackbed curves west on a shallow ledge cut into hillside as the Shrewsbury & Chester line drops to Dee viaduct (290432). *Acrefair*: Abutments of bridge over A539 Ruabon–Langollen road; Bridge over Rhos line (276432). *Trevor*: cleared station yard, apart from platforms on south side of same road. *Llangollen*: Few GWR stations have managed to survive as intact as this one for a decade after closure. Magnificent setting in town centre.* *Berwyn*: station buildings beside A5 (198432); Berwyn Tunnel (689yds), entrances heavily overgrown (189432); trackbed is within sight of the A5 virtually to Corwen. *Corwen*: station buildings. *Bala Junction*: station buildings (938355). *Bontnewydd*: signal box; *Dolgelley*: station (attractively Great Western) has been closed as long as Llangollen, but here vandals, as noted in the Barmouth Junction section, have shown more haste than the planners in deciding its immediate fate.

USES: *Corwen*: District Farmers' Association plans to erect a warehouse, offices and standing wharfage in station yard; objected to by Merioneth County Council at public inquiry in winter 1973. Now likely that the yard is to be developed partly for a by-pass and for a fire and ambulance station and industry. *Bala*: improvements to B4391 through demolition of overbridge and twisting approach (929349). Bala Lake Halt lay just west of the bridge. *Bontnewydd*: road widened and level crossing surfaced (770201). *Dolgelley*: GWR goods yard at west end of station used industrially; it is clearly visible from road bridge beside station, crossing wide and peaceful river Wnion, with which the Ruabon line kept company.

CHAPTER 5: GWR MOUNTAIN

BALA JUNCTION–BLAENAU FFESTINIOG   25½ miles
Great Western Railway

Although they met at Bala Junction, the Ffestiniog and Barmouth lines were noticeably different in character. The latter, which follows valleys from Ruabon, was a secondary route, while the generally short trains bound from Bala for the mountains, ran over what was never more than a branch. Rejoice that the northern section between Blaenau Ffestiniog and Trawsfynydd (Power Station) remains open. The siding used to tranship atomic waste containers lies 1¼ miles north of original Trawsfynydd station.

ACTS: 7 August 1862 Festiniog & Blaenau Railway (narrow gauge), 3½ miles. 13 April 1883: vested jointly in GWR and Bala & Festiniog Railway. 1 July 1910: GWR sole owner by amalgamation with Bala & Festiniog Railway. Bala & Festiniog Railway: 28 July 1873 (Incorporated). 27 March 1879: working agreement with GWR. 1 July 1910: Amalgamated with GWR.

OPENED: 30 May 1868: Festiniog & Blaenau: Ffestiniog–Duffws (Blaenau Ffestiniog), junction with Festiniog Railway. 10 September 1883: F & B converted to standard gauge. Bala & Festiniog Railway: 1 November 1882 Bala Junction (new station)–Ffestiniog. 10 September 1883: Ffestiniog–Blaenau Ffestiniog. 20 April 1964: new connection opened between LMS/GWR lines at Blaenau Ffestiniog to enable trains to reach Trawsfynydd nuclear power station over re-opened section.

CLOSED: 4 January 1960: Bala–Blaenau Ffestiniog (*Pass*); 28 January 1961: Bala–Blaenau Ffestiniog closed to local goods. 2 November 1964 Bala Junction–Bala (*Gds*); 18 January 1965 Bala Junction–Bala (*Pass*).

REMAINS: *Bala*: trackbed runs north from A494 (929363) and can be traced to Tryweryn Dam. *Capel Celyn*: road across Dam provides grandstand view of trackbed and valley far below, up which trains once pounded (879401).* Reservoir submerged nearly two miles of track, but bed appears again (857399) and its course can be traced from the B4391 on the opposite side of the lake. *Cwm Prysor*: curved arch viaduct (the major engineering work) survives on a lonely, but accessible, mountainside (778388).* From it the trackbed runs on to a spectacular ledge high above the main road. *Ffestiniog*: dilapidated goods shed and more dilapidated station buildings and signal box. *Manod*: trackbed of original narrow gauge Festiniog & Blaenau Railway lies in a field beside stone viaduct carrying the existing line (706453);* *Blaenau Ffestiniog*: amid the now-levelled yard, platform used by GWR and Festiniog Railway passenger trains, the line to Trawsfynydd runs through derelict station yard.

USES: *Bala*: station and yard redeveloped as industrial estate plus easily-spotted new fire station, and car park. A494 improved by demolition of station and road overbridge at northern end of platforms. *Frongoch*: station now a house (903391); *Capel Celyn*: trackbed drowned by Liverpool Corporation Reservoir (see *Remains*). *Arenig*: granite company has extended workings across trackbed. Main road across the mountains (B4391) realigned on trackbed for short distance (792383). Half-mile east of station, trackbed converted to a private road, continuing east and utilising railway bridge over Nant Aberderfel (850394). *Trawsfynydd*: station house privately occupied; yard used by coal merchant (710372). *Maentwrog Road*: station in private use (695398). *Tanymanod*: station yard and locomotive shed site used for housing (705452).

CHAPTER 6: GWR BY ADOPTION: CAMBRIAN DELIGHTS

OSWESTRY–WELSHPOOL   15½ miles
Oswestry & Newtown Railway

Compensation here for the motorist because the A483, which parallels the old line, offers the same fine views of a hill- and crag-flanked section of the Severn Valley.

ACT: 26 June 1855. Cambrian Railways from 25 July 1864.
OPENED: 1 May 1860 Oswestry–Pool Quay; 14 August 1860 Pool Quay–Welshpool.

CLOSED: 18 January 1965 Llynclys Junction–Welshpool (*Pass* and *Gds*).

Note: Oswestry lost its last passenger service to Gobowen on 7 November 1966, when the intermediate Park Hall Halt closed. The former Cambrian and GWR goods depots at Oswestry amalgamated at Grouping. They closed 6 December 1971.

REMAINS: *Oswestry*: for details see Chapter 6. *Llanymynech*: overgrown station site, (including junction with Shropshire & Montgomeryshire Railway); cylindrical piers and abutments of O & N bridge over river Vyrnwy (271205): but note that while they did allow for double track, the main line was always single.

USES: *Pool Quay*: trackbed used to straighten A483. Countryside Commission report *Disused Railways in the Countryside of England and Wales* suggested that the railway embankment near Pool Quay could be a useful farm stock refuge when the Severn flooded.

OSWESTRY–WHITCHURCH   18¼ miles
Oswestry Ellesmere & Whitchurch Railway

Grandstand views from road overbridges remain at Welshampton and Frankton, showing the totally rural character of the line through gently rolling country, lush and green, that gets a little hillier towards Oswestry, with its backcloth of the Welsh hills.

ACT: 1 August 1861: part of Cambrian Railways from 25 July 1864.
OPENED: Whitchurch–Ellesmere: 20 April 1863 (*Gds*); 4 May 1863 (*Pass*); Ellesmere–Oswestry: 27 July 1864 (*Pass* and *Gds*).
CLOSED: 18 January 1965 (*Pass*); 29 March 1965 (*Gds*).
REMAINS: *Whittington*: bridge abutments over Shrewsbury–Chester line—OE & W trackbed on embankment. *Park Hall*: bridge abutments at sharp S-bend on Oswestry–Whitchurch main road. *Whitchurch*: Junction with Shrewsbury & Crewe line just south of station. Trackbed clearly definable curving sharply west.
USES: *Welshampton*: station now a house (440357); *Frankton*: station now a house. Cambrian Coat of Arms in engraved brick suggests it was possibly the company house occupied by a senior official (365345).* *Ellesmere*: station yard developed into large industrial estate with modern buildings in contrast to original station block. Shallow cutting and embankments leading to road overbridges effectively shield the factories from surroundings that are rural on

all but the south (town) side. *Whitchurch*: LNWR turntable, used by OE & W locomotives, disused from 1965. Dismantled and transferred to Severn Valley Railway, Bridgnorth in 1974.

WREXHAM–ELLESMERE   12¾ miles
Wrexham & Ellesmere Railway

A line that lacked the rugged character of other GWR branches around Wrexham, and also many of those of its parent, the Cambrian Railways. Only 1½ miles between Wrexham and brickworks remain open.

ACT: 31 July 1885. Worked by Cambrian Railways from opening. Absorbed by GWR at Grouping.

OPENED: 2 November 1895.

CLOSED: 10 September 1962 (*Pass*); also Ellesmere–Pickhill (*Gds*); Pickhill–Wrexham outskirts: summer 1973 (*Gds*).

REMAINS: *Bangor-on-Dee*: Two platforms, signal box and goods shed (399456), abutments of (removed) bridge across river Dee and approach embankments (397463).

USES: Denbighshire County Council was recommended to purchase section closed 1973 so as to ensure suitable disposal of the land. The County Planning Officer did not consider the section had any scenic value for footpath or country park.

PORTHYWAEN–LLANGYNOG   14 miles
Tanat Valley Light Railway

A light railway with small traffic which never achieved the status of its neighbour serving Llanfyllin, market town and railhead for a much wider area than that around Llangynog.

ACT: 4 June 1899 Light Railway Order. Cambrian Railways worked the line from opening, and absorbed the company 12 March 1921.

OPENED: 5 January 1904.

CLOSED: 15 January 1951: Llynclys Junction–Llangynog (*Pass*); 1 July 1952: Llanrhaiadr Mochnant–Llangynog (*Gds*); 5 December 1960: Blodwell Junction–Llanrhaiadr Mochnant (*Gds*). Llynclys–Blodwell Junction retained for Nantmawr quarry trains.

REMAINS: Trackbed sections. *Llanrhaiadr Mochnant*: station buildings (134249); *Penybontfawr*: station goods yard for sale 1974 with planning permission for four bungalows (090248). *Llangynog*: station buildings, goods shed and passenger and goods platforms.

GAZETTEER

USES: *Llanrhaiadr Mochnant*: level crossing just east of station eliminated by improvements on Llanfyllin road (B4580).

LLANYMYNECH–LLANFYLLIN   8¼ miles
Oswestry & Newtown Railway

The Llanfyllin branch was the Cambrian Railways' most substantial branch in the Border country since it was operated as a conventional branch, while its neighbour to the north, the Tanat Valley, was a Light Railway, and the Welshpool & Llanfair to the south, was narrow gauge.

ACT: 17 May 1861.
OPENED: 17 July 1863.
CLOSED: 27 January 1896: Rock Siding–Wern. Llanymynech–
    Rock Siding (*Pass*); August 1914 (*Gds*); Wern–Llanfyllin: 2
    November 1964 (*Gds*); 18 January 1965 (*Pass*). Also connection
    (opened 27 January 1896) Wern–Nantmawr Junction.
REMAINS: *Llanymynech*: original branch route via Rock Siding can
    be traced by banks of Shropshire Union Canal (271211). See also
    note in Oswestry–Welshpool section. *Carreghofa*: railway and canal
    bridged by B4398. *Llansantffraid*: signal box which controlled level
    crossing (the only one on the branch) preserved in situ.
USES: *Llansantffraid*: station adapted as restaurant. Goods shed in
    main street nearby. Main road bend eased and banked across
    trackbed at west end of village. *Llanfyllin*: station in commercial
    use with overall roof across platform and trackbed to goods shed.

LLANYMYNECH–NANTMAWR   4 miles
Shrewsbury & North Wales Railway

Few branch lines, even those of similarly remote rural areas, suffered more ups and downs, yet part remains to serve Nantmawr quarries.

ACT: 7 May 1862. Became Potteries, Shrewsbury & North Wales
    Railway: 16 July 1866; became Shropshire Railways: 7 August
    1888. Worked by Cambrian Railways from 1 June 1881.
OPENED & CLOSED: 13 August 1866 (*Gds*). Closed: 21 December
    1866–1868 (*Gds*). Re-opened: 1868 (*Gds*). Passenger service for
    the first time: 18 April 1870. Closed: 22 June 1880 (*All traffic*);
    Re-opened: 1 June 1881 (*Gds*); 5 January 1904 (*Pass*). Final
    closures: 1 January 1917 Nantmawr Junction (Carreghofa)–
    Blodwell Junction (*Pass*); 1925 (*Gds*); 2 November 1964 (*Gds*);

134

18 January 1965 (*Pass*). Passenger services between Llanymy-nech–Blodwell Junction only.

REMAINS: *Llanyblodwell*: bridge piers across river Tanat (249227); main road (A495) bridges river and trackbed beside (250221); *Carreghofa*: river bridge abutments (253218).

USES: *Blodwell Junction*: Station derelict, but former passing loop used as run-round by Gobowen–Nantmawr stone trains. Blodwell Junction–Nantmawr officially open, but only short length used (253231). Ungated crossing across A495 (257235).

ABERMULE–KERRY   3¾ miles
Oswestry & Newtown Railway

Branches were never more rural than this, a perfect subject for the meticulous modeller. Animate a layout with Dean 0–6–0s, among the last locomotives to use the line.

ACT: 17 May 1861.
OPENED: 2 March 1863 (*Pass*); 1 July 1863 (*Gds*).
CLOSED: 9 February 1931 (*Pass*); 1 May 1956 (*Gds*).
REMAINS: *Fronfraith*: bridge carrying minor road over river Mule and trackbed through station site (166935).
USES: *Kerry*: station privately occupied (163903).

BARMOUTH JUNCTION–DOLGELLAU   7¾ miles
Aberystwyth & Welsh Coast Railway

This short and lovely line is so easy to remember as nothing other than part of the GWR route from Ruabon to the sea, yet for more than 50 of its 90-odd year existence, it was pure Cambrian.

ACT: 29 July 1862. Absorbed by CR 5 July 1865 (half-completed).
OPENED: 3 July 1865: Barmouth Junction–Penmaenpool; 21 June 1869 Penmaenpool–Dolgellau.
CLOSED: 14 December 1964 (*Gds*); 18 January 1965 (*Pass*). Morfa Mawddach: 4 November 1963 (*Gds*).
REMAINS: *Morfa Mawddach*: buildings of station (unstaffed, like many Cambrian Coast line stations since 1 March 1965) demolished August 1974. Dolgellau branch platform trackless. Route of east to south curve, which completed triangle, easy to trace. *Penmaenpool*: locomotive shed. Concrete platform ribs and signals still in position 1973 at approach to road toll bridge (695184).* Station buildings in private use. *Dolgellau*: station and signal box derelict early 1974.

USES: Merioneth County Council has bought trackbed and plans to adapt five miles Barmouth Junction–Penmaenpool as public footpath, with car parks laid to serve it.

MOAT LANE–TALYLLYN   56 miles
Mid Wales Railway

Much of the trackbed remains, a delightfully scenic memorial to the promoters who took the line to almost 1,000ft above sea level without major engineering works on the scale of others that reached similar heights.

ACTS: Moat Lane–Llanidloes: 4 June 1853 (as part of the Llanidloes & Newtown Railway); Llanidloes–Newbridge: 1 August 1859; Newbridge–Talyllyn Junction: 3 July 1860; Builth Road Curve to LNWR: 30 June 1864. MWR worked by Cambrian Railways from 2 April 1888.

OPENED: Moat Lane–Llanidloes: 30 April 1859 (*Gds*); 2 September 1859 (*Pass*): L & N Railway. Llanidloes–Talyllyn: 1 September 1864 (*Gds*); 21 September 1864 (*Pass*). Builth Road Curve to LNWR: 1 November 1866. Curve sold to LNWR 4 July 1870.

CLOSED: Moat Lane–Talyllyn: 31 December 1962 (*Pass*); also Llanidloes–Talyllyn (*Gds*). Moat Lane–Llanidloes retained until 2 October 1967 for cement to Clywedog Reservoir, six miles long, in the hills near Llanidloes. Builth Road Curve used for goods to Builth Road (Low Level) until 6 September 1965.

REMAINS: *Moat Lane*: Original Llanidloes & Newtown station at Caersws, ¼-mile to the south (028918) outlives, as a house, the more imposing junction station in the 'middle-of-nowhere' (042911), opened to serve the main line. The junction station buildings have been demolished, although a derelict platform remains. *Dolwen*: station buildings (also L & N) privately occupied. *Llanidloes*: easy to put memory's clock back to 1962 and before when the station and yard, with goods shed and a larger one for locomotives, were really busy. All remain—the shapely station building as engineering company offices, the yard in industrial use.* *Tylwch*: station is a private house (970801); *Pantydwr*: station just south of MWR summit 947ft, also privately owned (983746); *St Harmons*: station site used for housing (989718); *Rhayader*: County Council owns station and maintains buildings; about two miles of the trackbed will be used for a Rhayader by-pass from the A44 just north of the town to the A470; *Doldowlod*: station site used for hotel (988628); *Newbridge*: station site developed for housing (015584); *Builth Road (Low Level)*: station and buildings adapted as basis of industrial complex straggling trackbed south of station (easily noted from Central Wales trains)*; Compare page 107 with *Cambrian Railways* Vol. 1 Christiansen/Miller, page 128. *Builth Wells*: level crossing at north of station and platform ends swallowed by large roundabout; *Three Cocks*: much-photographed junction (with Hereford Hay & Brecon), now filled-in to platform level by bottle-gas company, which has supplemented station buildings (167372). Trackbed locally adapted for realignment of South Wales trunk road (A479). *Brecon*: station which Mid Wales Railway shared with Brecon & Merthyr and other companies is now demolished.

PENPONTBREN JUNCTION–LLANGURIG   3 miles
Manchester & Milford Railway

In a sense the most unforgotten of branches, because virtually all the earthworks remain undisturbed, for this is one of the most remote and loveliest sections of the Wye Valley.

ACT: 23 July 1860: Llanidloes–Pencader (approximately 50 miles).
OPENED: Penpontbren–Llangurig completed by February 1864 but used only by one goods train. Line abandoned after the M & M modified plans to Aberystwyth.
REMAINS: Trackbed easy to follow to Llangurig, where an original bridge spans minor road (908799). Trackbed ends in field. Traces of any further construction that might have been carried out is obliterated by mature Forestry Commission plantation.

ELAN VALLEY RAILWAY   Approximately 7 miles

Although hardly built to branch line standards, this contractors' line was well engineered into the valley and surrounding hills. What a preserved railway it might have become had it survived until today. Perhaps if it had not closed during a world war the tourist-conscious Cambrian might have considered buying and developing part as a scenic branch. There is nothing in the Board minutes to suggest that it ever thought about it.

ACT: 27 June 1892. Built by contractor of Birmingham Corporation, Lovatt of Wolverhampton.
OPENED: 1894.
CLOSED: October 1916: Final 2½ miles: Noyadd Sidings–Caban Coch Dam. 23 February 1917: Elan Valley Junction–Noyadd (½ mile).

REMAINS: Trackbed can be traced from near Dolfallen bridge over river Elan (955665) to Caban Coch.

USES: Much of the original system dismantled as dams were completed. In 1974 the Water Resources Board said that it was considering enlarging Craig Coch into Britain's biggest reservoir.

CAERSWS–VAN   6½ miles
Van Railway

Mountainy! You will either get sunburnt or soaked searching for the Van's remains on Plynlimon's slopes, where the weather remains as individual as the railway was. Nothing but mines could have induced anyone to build a railway in such exposed country.

ACT: None. 22 May 1873: adapted for passenger working under Board of Trade Certificate. 1 August 1896: worked by Cambrian Railways. 1 January 1923: absorbed by GWR.
OPENED: 14 August 1871 (*Gds*); 1 December 1873 (*Pass*).
CLOSED: 1879 (*Pass*); 1893 (*Gds*). Re-opened by CR 1 August 1896.
REMAINS: *Van*: station buildings (951874). Although mine buildings have been demolished, the site of the mines are clearly visible.
USES: *Caersws*: old Van Railway station and locomotive shed form part of BR Engineers' Depot on down side of Cambrian main line.

CEMMES ROAD–DINAS MAWDDWY   6¾ miles
The Mawddwy Railway

Like the Van Railway, privately-built and highly individual. It served an area remote and self-contained. Also revived by the Cambrian Railways (helped by enlightened local authorities) after initial failure.

ACT: 5 July 1865. Worked by Cambrian Railways from 31 July 1911. Absorbed by GWR at Grouping.
OPENED: 1 October 1867.
CLOSED: 17 April 1901 (*Pass*); 8 April 1908 (*Gds*). Re-opened: 31 July 1911. Finally closed: 1 January 1931 (*Pass*); 1 July 1951 (*Gds*: last train ran 5 September 1950).
REMAINS: *Cemmes Road*: trackbed can be noted curving north from Cambrian main line (822045); *Aberangell*: shapely arch bridge over river Angell: one of the few engineering works on the line (845100).

USES: *Dinas Mawddwy*: Trackbed developed for narrow gauge line (page 16) running 600yd to picnic area. Steam operated.

ABERDOVEY HARBOUR BRANCH   Approximately ½ mile
Aberystwyth & Welsh Coast Railway

Aberdovey was the Cambrian's busiest port, and for a few months in 1889 it maintained a passenger service to Waterford with two paddle steamers.

ACT: 22 July 1861. Became part of the CR 5 July 1865.
OPENED: 24 October 1863.
CLOSED: 14 August 1867 (*Pass*); 4 May 1964 (*Gds*).
USES: The quay warehouse built by the *Railways* proclaims Aberdovey's maritime history in a museum created by the Outward Bound Trust. Next door is Merioneth's first National Park Centre, opened July 1972 on the old coal wharf. It contains several railway photographs.

CHAPTER 7: LNWR SNOWDONIA

PENYGROES–NANTLLE   1½ miles

Short, but historic. By far the most interesting of the branches between Bangor and Afon Wen.

ACT: 20 May 1825 (for 3ft 6in gauge tramway, horse-worked, from Nantlle to Carnarvon, 9¼ miles). 25 July 1867: Carnarvonshire Railway given authority to convert to standard gauge Pengroes–Nantlle, and abandon Penygroes–Carnarvon, while retaining section between Nantlle and local quarries as tramroad.
OPENED: 1828: Nantlle–Carnarvon tramroad. 1 October 1872: Penygroes–Nantlle opened as standard gauge line.
CLOSED: 22 February 1872: Carnarvon Quay narrow gauge lines; 8 August 1932: Penygroes–Nantlle (*Pass*); 2 December 1963 (*Gds*).
USES: Few branches have been re-developed as comprehensively as this; few as well. *Nantlle*: station building retained in private use while the railway yard (site of two gauge interchange sidings) has been replaced by tourists' car park and children's play area, landscaped and fenced. Careful, overall planning has toned-down eyesores of the past and provided a fresh, pleasant environment (488529). Much trackbed used to build a road to carry tourists, who have replaced slate quarrying as the local industry, clear of

the narrow, twisting main street of the village. The new road runs between Nantlle and the eastern outskirts of Penygroes, but it is likely that more of the branch will be used to extend it to the Caernarvon road. That will leave only a small section of trackbed derelict, and also Penygroes station, where land reclamation is planned. *Penygroes*: station building, goods shed and signal box much vandalised, but platforms intact; *Chwilog*: station building and platform intact. Level crossing gates still in place on B4354.

MENAI BRIDGE–AFON WEN   25¾ miles
London & North Western Railway

Another secondary route to the Cambrian coast, very much Euston's answer to Paddington's route from Ruabon. Neither line was used by many people, except at holiday times.

ACTS: 20 May 1851: Bangor & Carnarvon Railway; 1852: leased to Chester & Holyhead Railway; 1 January 1859: C & H, including Bangor & Carnarvon, amalgamated with LNWR; B & C vested in LNWR 15 July 1867. 29 July 1862: Carnarvonshire Railway; 1869: absorbed by LNWR.

OPENED: 1 March 1852: Menai Bridge Junction–Port Dinorwic (*Gds*); 1 July 1852: Menai Bridge–Carnarvon (*Pass*); 2 September 1867: Carnarvon (Pant)–Afon Wen (*Pass & Gds*); 5 July 1870: Carnarvon Town line linking Pant station with terminus of Bangor & Carnarvon. 1 August 1870: Carnarvon Harbour branch.

CLOSED: 1 August 1870: Carnarvon (Pant) closed (*Pass*); 5 July 1937: Griffith's Crossing, Carnarvon (*Pass*); 10 September 1951: Dinas station (*Pass & Gds*); 10 September 1951: Pantglas (*Pass*); 2 March 1957: Treborth (*Pass*); 11 September 1960: Port Dinorwic (*Pass*); 7 December 1964: line closure Carnarvon–Afon Wen (*Pass & Gds*); 5 January 1970: Carnarvon–Menai Bridge (*Pass*). Menai Bridge–Carnarvon 5 February 1972 (*Gds*). Caernarvon LMS engine shed had closed 14 September 1931.

REMAINS: Trackbed can be traced most of the way. From Menai Bridge it runs through trees beside small (overgrown) marshalling yard on the down side of the C & H main line, near approach curve to Britannia Bridge. *Caernarvon*: viaduct south of tunnel (482620).

USES: Gwynedd County Council, which owned already the trackbed between Afon Wen and Pont Seiont, Caernarvon, purchased a further 6½ miles, comprising 69 acres, from there to a point north of Pont Ty Golchi for £133,700 in 1974, assuming responsibility for bridges, crossings of the trackbed, walls, embankments and fences. The County Council stated that it might sell trackbed that it does not need; about the same time it was reported that an undefined straight section may be used by a brake manufacturing firm to speed-test products. *Menai Bridge*: station used as offices and store. *Pont Ty Golchi*: road improvements included demolition of accident-prone railway bridge over A4087 on 8 December 1974. *Port Dinorwic*: station buildings now offices. Railway bridge with twisting approaches demolished 8 December 1974 (525674) and railway land may be used for holiday flats development. *Griffith's Crossing–Caernarvon*: trackbed to be used for improved road between Caernarvon proposed inner ring road and a projected by-pass at Port Dinorwic. *Caernarvon*: Station site to be developed for light industry, possibly also for commercial and residential schemes. Trackbed through town centre (including Y Maes Tunnel (164yd), likely to be converted into road for light traffic only because of ventilation, flooding, and clearance problems. Section of line just south, near Castle, is an extended car park. *Dinas Junction*: LNWR platforms intact, together with stone building on the down siding, but wooden LNWR buildings including signal box have gone. The Welsh Highland Railway section of the yard and its buildings are a council depot and the trackbed under a road bridge is used by vehicles to get between different sections of the depot. *Llanwnda*: Station building intact. Yard used by coal merchant. *Afon Wen*: station, only one to be closed on Cambrian Coast line, offered for sale in 1973. Section north for some miles towards Caernarvon likely to be developed for pony-trekking.

PORT DINORWIC (PORT SIDING)–PORT SIDING   1 mile
London & North Western Railway

Traffic originating from this branch (and that to the other 'slate' port of Penrhyn, just north of Bangor), must have well repaid Euston for its trouble in constructing such short lines.

ACT: None.
OPENED: c. 1857.
CLOSED: 12 September 1960 (*Gds* only).
REMAINS: *Port Dinorwic*: bridge carrying Bangor–Caernarvon road (A499) over trackbed where it runs into the port, beside small dock (527678).

USES: The trackbed inside the Port to slate dock was to be used by marina being developed.

CAERNARVON–LLANBERIS   9 miles
London & North Western Railway

Trains from Caernarvon—there were many summer excursions after the line closed to local passenger trains—pounded through narrow, twisting valleys to emerge into the foothills around Llanberis, rather like surfacing submarines.

ACT: 14 July 1864: Carnarvon & Llanberis Railway.
OPENED: 1 July 1869.
CLOSED: 22 September 1930: end of regular passenger services.
7 September 1964: end of excursion traffic and closure to *Gds*.
REMAINS: Trackbed easy to trace.
USES: *Caernarvon*: trackbed in the vicinity of Eryri Hospital on the outskirts developed for industry (485615); Cwm-y-Glo: track earmarked for local by-pass (555623); *Llanberis*: final mile of line past passenger station (standing) to goods depot converted into by-pass.*

BANGOR (BETHESDA JUNCTION)–BETHESDA   4¼ miles
London & North Western Railway

The branch's fortunes would have been much different had it carried the slate traffic that was the monopoly of the narrow gauge Padarn Railway, with which it kept company for a short distance.

ACT: 6 August 1880.
OPENED: 1 July 1884 (*Pass*); 1 September 1884 (*Gds*).
CLOSED: 3 December 1951 (*Pass*); 7 October 1963 (*Gds*).
USES: *Bethesda*: part of station yard will be incorporated into by-pass to take the Holyhead Road (A5) clear of the busy main street. The rest may be used for light industry and a club. *Tregarth*: trackbed has been merged into a playing field and footpath to main road. Tregarth–Bethesda may become the basis of a footpath system through delightful country that motorists will never know—unless they are encouraged to stop and alight.

BANGOR (PENRHYN SIDINGS)–PENRHYN QUAY   1½ miles
Chester & Holyhead Railway

ACT:
OPENED: February 1852 (minerals only).
CLOSED: 30 June 1965; Penrhyn Sidings Ground Frame, Bethesda

Page 143 Demoted junction. *(Above)* Coed Talon, between Mold and Brymbo, was once the junction for the Ffrith branch, which ran in along the overgrown trackbed on the left, past the single-storey wagon works, which are still standing.

(Below) The LNWR village station at Coed Talon in April 1959. Ex-LMS Class 4 0–6–0 44065 of Mold Junction shed pauses with the daily goods. On this occasion with a second brake van for Branch Line Society members.

Page 144 Pastoral Wales. *(Above)* Bodfari, where the station remains but the overbridge has been demolished to improve the main road. Scenically, LNWR lines between Chester – Corwen – Rhyl were vastly different to those in Snowdonia.

(Below) Ex-LMS Class 4 2–6–4T No 42461 stands at Mold with an RCTS Special in October 1955. But for the initiative of the railway societies, many enthusiasts would never have traversed these now-closed branches.

Junction, taken out of use 2 March 1963. Penrhyn Sidings Box had closed 23 August 1954.

REMAINS: Trackbed at approach to privately-owned dock (591725).

USES: *Port Penrhyn*: designated as industrial site. Road access good. Site will include utilisation of lines within the Port (narrow and standard gauge). Area beside C & H main line and branch near junction designated as open space (589711).

SETTING: Branch ran through green and wooded valley on outskirts of Bangor close to Penrhyn Castle. Good view of Port Penrhyn from minor road (591725).

HOLLAND ARMS–RED WHARF BAY   6¾ miles
London & North Western Railway

When the LMS decided to abandon passenger services in 1930, the holiday popularity of this part of Anglesey was still some years away.

ACTS: 1 August 1899 and 6 August 1900.

OPENED: 1 July 1909: Holland Arms–Pentraeth; 24 May 1909: Pentraeth–Red Wharf Bay.

CLOSED: 22 September 1930 (*Pass*); 3 April 1950 (*Gds*); 4 August 1952: Holland Arms station closed.

REMAINS: Trackbed easily traced. *Holland Arms*: station buildings (471725). Station building used as offices; yard as coal store. *Pentraeth*: high embankment and cuttings.

CHAPTER 8: LNWR NORTH EAST WALES

SALTNEY FERRY (Mold Junction No 3 Box)–MOLD   10 miles
The Mold Railway

Not least of the pleasures of a rail journey between Chester and Mold was the climb from the junction to the hill-locked valley onwards from Penyffordd, a bank that made LMS Class 2 4–4–0s sing and cry for many years. Penyffordd–Mold (Synthite Sidings) still has a daily goods and in 1974 special trains began running to a depot for pipes being delivered for the Amlwch–Stanlow oil pipeline at Rhydymwyn.

ACT: 9 July 1847
OPENED: 14 August 1849.

CLOSED: 6 January 1958: Padeswood & Buckley (*Pass*); 1 September 1958: Hope Exchange (High and Low Levels); 30 April 1962: Denbigh–Mold–Chester (*Pass*); 2 September 1963: Workmen's specials Chester–Broughton & Bretton (retained from end of through passenger service); 1 March 1965: Mold Junction–Penyffordd (*Gds*).

REMAINS: *Mold Junction*: locomotive depot (LMS 6B) which provided power for the branch, closed 18 April 1966. Now a derelict shell. *Broughton & Bretton*: station buildings beside A55 (350642); *Penyffordd*: earthworks of unbuilt south-to-east spur with Wrexham Mold & Connah's Quay at High Level (295614).

USES: *Mold Junction*: branch curves away from the still quite busy marshalling yard, of which it now forms a siding.
Mold: Modern notices warn: Beware of trains. Stop! Look! Listen! That is because after ten years of being semi-derelict the station has been taken over by builders' merchants. The notices are needed because trains still run through to Rhydymwyn.

MOLD–DENBIGH   15¾ miles
Mold & Denbigh Junction Railway

As scenic and true a secondary line as any in Britain. Mainly double-tracked with a passenger service of double the average branch line intensity, the line gave a busy rural area based on the market towns of Mold and Denbigh a quick link with Chester.

ACT: 6 August 1861.
OPENED: 12 September 1869.
CLOSED: 30 April 1962: Mold–Denbigh (*Pass*) and Rhydymwyn (Dolfechlas Crossing) (205675)–Denbigh (*Gds*). Mold–Rhydymwyn re-opened freight 13 July 1974.
REMAINS: *Rhydymwyn*: station buildings (207668); *Nannerch*: wall that separated railway from main road (A541) to prevent fright to horse-drawn vehicles (153705); *Star Crossing*: station buildings (177679); *Caerwys*: station buildings (127716); *Bodfari*: station buildings (095699) and short length of earthworks of unbuilt west-to-north curve with Vale of Clwyd (068698); *Denbigh*: station buildings.
USES: *Nannerch*: station buildings were converted into private house with garden created in fill-in area between platforms. Later the house was demolished to eliminate sharp S-bend and over-bridge on A541 (169691); *Bodfari*: same road—overbridge demolished and hump taken out of road. *Denbigh*: Part of station

146

yard used for road improvements. Goods and locomotive shed in commercial use on small industrial estate developed in station yard.

RHYL (FORYD) JUNCTION–DENBIGH   10 miles
Vale of Clwyd Railway

The 'daddy' of local lines which lost some importance and traffic when the Chester–Denbigh–Corwen line opened. A single 'mood-changing' branch that took southbound passengers away from the delights of wide-promenaded Rhyl into the quiet of this Welsh vale.

ACT: 23 June 1856. Extension of 1 mile to Foryd Pier, Rhyl, authorised by LNWR Act 30 June 1862. VOC absorbed by LNWR 1867.
OPENED: 5 October 1858.
CLOSED: 20 April 1885: Foryd Station (*Pass*); 19 September 1955: Rhyl–Denbigh (*Pass*), and Denbigh locomotive shed; 6 April 1959: Rhyl (Foryd)–Foryd Pier (Rhyl Harbour branch); 1 January 1968: Rhyl–Denbigh (*Gds*).
REMAINS: *Foryd Pier*: typical LNWR timber goods warehouse. *Foryd*: remains of level crossing over main coast road. Trackbed easy to trace from Chester & Holyhead main line, which it passes under just after branch trackbed curves south beyond station (994801).
USES: *St Asaph*: trackbed severed by motorway-style by-pass of A55 (038749); *Trefnant*: A541 overbridge with sharp, steep east approach demolished—road levelled and improved, utilising part of single platform (053707). Station yard redeveloped with bungalows. *Denbigh*: part of trackbed to be used for by-pass on Pentrefoelas–Rhyl main road.

RHYL (FORYD SIDINGS)–KINMEL PARK   4 miles
War Department

Built for the needs of war the line, which originally served a big army camp, survived several decades as a peace-time mineral outlet from a limestone quarry.

ACT: None.
OPENED: During World War I.
CLOSED: February 1965.
REMAINS: *St George*: level crossing on A55 (982761).

DENBIGH–CORWEN   18¾ miles
Denbigh, Ruthin & Corwen Railway
This was a line that served the middle and upper Vale of Clwyd
and its people. Except perhaps between Denbigh and Ruthin one
would find mainly local people among its passengers, for few ever
thought of going from Corwen to Chester, except through Wrexham.
That was by *Great* Western. The Denbigh route was *North* Western—
but for those who can remember it with affection, none the worse
for that.

ACT: 23 July 1860: DR & C absorbed by LNWR 1879.
OPENED: 1 March 1862: Denbigh–Ruthin; September 1864:
Ruthin–Corwen: junction with Llangollen & Corwen from 1
September 1865.
CLOSED: 2 February 1953: Ruthin–Corwen (*Pass*. Retained for
excursion traffic until 8 September 1961); 30 April 1962: Denbigh
–Ruthin (*Pass*), and Ruthin–Corwen (*Gds*); 1 March 1965:
Denbigh–Ruthin (*Gds*).
REMAINS: *Eyarth*: station now a house (130555); *Corwen*: curved
trackbed in fields of Dee Valley (075444).
USES: *Ruthin*: station buildings demolished and land used for by-
pass, including large roundabout.

HOLYWELL JUNCTION–HOLYWELL TOWN   1¼ miles
London & North Western Railway
Holywell Junction station, closed to passengers 14 February 1966,
is the only Victorian station in Wales to be scheduled for preservation, yet it did not get its junction status until 1912. It is worth
remembering if one goes in search of so short a line, that even as
recently as the early 1900s, the North Western regarded it as
financially worthwhile to build. And everything seems to suggest
that it helped the development of the steep valley and brought a
better standard of living to its people.

ACTS: 29 July 1864: Holywell Railway Company authorised to
build two-mile line between town and small harbour, with link
to Chester & Holyhead main line. 13 July 1868: scheme abandoned. 20 July 1906: LNWR authorised to construct Holywell
curve and build a branch.
OPENED: 1 July 1912.
CLOSED: 6 September 1954: All traffic except Holywell Junction–

Crescent Siding at Holywell Textile Mills (¼-mile); 11 August 1967: branch closed completely.

REMAINS: *Holywell*: trackbed and cutting leading to station site.

USES: *Holywell*: station and yard which lay in deep cutting, partly filled-in and yard converted into road and car park.

FFRITH JUNCTION–LLANFYNYDD (Joint Line
    Junction): FFRITH BRANCH   3½ miles
Chester & Holyhead Railway

This really is a forgotten railway. It closed more than 40 years ago and everything that it was built to serve, notably mines and quarries around Coed Talon, have gone, or use other forms of transport.

ACT: 9 July 1847.
OPENED: 14 September 1849: Ffrith Junction–Coed Talon. Later extended to Llanfynydd, where the junction with the Wrexham & Minera Extension Joint Railway opened 27 January 1872 (see Chapter 2).
CLOSED: 29 July 1934 (*Gds*—no passenger service).
REMAINS: Trackbed lies in dense woods beside A5104, through twisting valley climbing steeply towards Coed Talon. *Leeswood*: on bridge over track, lifted 1936, narrowest (and steepest) of by-roads (278603); *Coed Talon*: trackbed can be traced beyond 'Railway Inn' running past village school towards Joint Line Junction and Brymbo (270586).
USES: *Coed Talon*: junction and sidings of station yard obliterated by road widening to improve access to Leeswood Village (269589). Station yard used by transport company and as extended car park for 'Railway Inn'. Former wagon works split in two and converted into houses.

COED TALON–MOLD (Tryddyn Junction)   4¼ miles
London & North Western Railway

Passengers could see little of the pleasant country through which the line passed because it ran virtually all the way in deep cutting.

ACT: None. Built privately to serve collieries. 16 July 1866: LNWR Act for new (and adapted) line Coed Talon–Mold; 13 May 1868: Transferred to LNWR.
OPENED: 8 July 1870–Rebuilt and extended line to Mold. 1 January 1892: (*Pass*).

CLOSED: 27 March 1950 (*Pass*); 22 July 1963 (*Gds*).

REMAINS: *Nercwys*: Trackbed in deep cutting (245615); *Mold*: abutments of bridge that carried branch over Wrexham road: A541 (244628).

BRYMBO–LLANFYNYDD   3 miles
Wrexham & Minera Extension Joint Railway

More rural and delightful than one could expect of any adjunct of routes through a major coal, steel and quarrying area. The quarries it served never grew to over-scar the green, steep-sided valley.

ACT: 5 July 1865. Leased to GWR & LNWR: 11 June 1866. GWR/LMS Joint: 1923–48.

OPENED: 27 January 1872 (*Gds*); 15 November 1897 (*Pass*).

CLOSED: 27 March 1950 (*Pass*); 1 January 1951: Coed Talon–Bwlchgwyn Siding (*Gds*); 1 October 1963: Bwlchgwyn Siding–Brymbo (*Gds*).

REMAINS: *Brymbo*: platform and site of junction with Minera line (297538). At Wrexham end of platform, trackbed of short siding where branch passenger trains (to Mold) stabled. *Ffrith*: five-arch stone viaduct (only major engineering work) overshadows new housing estate (284552). *Llanfynydd*: long trackbed stretch overlooked by Offa's Dyke (280563).

USES: *Broughton*: acute, steeply-graded bend on B5101 road eliminated 1972–3 by demolishing part of railway embankment and iron overbridge (296544). Remains of embankment (graded 1 in 40) lie to west of road.

Bibliography

This is a selection of books about railways in North and Mid Wales. It is not exhaustive, for most guide books contain references to them. They do not always show railways in too favourable a light; even the scenery could become boring if connections at country stations were lengthy. Search for comments in old guides can be rewarding.

Books containing useful bibliographies that point to further sources are indicated by an asterisk (*).

Background Books

Appleton, J. H. *Disused Railways in the Countryside of England and Wales* (1970)*. A report to the Countryside Commission
Baxter, B. *Stone Blocks & Iron Rails* (1966)*
Biddle, G. *Victorian Railway Stations*
Bradley, V. J. and Hindley, P. (editors). *Industrial and Independent Locomotives and Railways of North Wales* (Birmingham Locomotive Club 1968)*
Bradshaw. *Shareholders' Guides and Timetables*
Casserley, H. C. *Railway History in Pictures: Wales & the Welsh Border Counties*
Clinker, C. R. *Register of Closed Passenger Stations and Goods Depots in England, Scotland and Wales*
Daniels, G. and Dench, L. A. *Passengers No More* (second edition 1973)
Lewthwaite, G. C. *Branch Line Index* (second edition 1971 and supplements)

Lyons, E. *An Historical Survey of GWR Engine Sheds 1947*
Railway Clearing House. *Railway Junction Diagrams*, 1915
Railway Clearing House. *Handbook of Stations*
Ramblers' Association. *Rural Transport in Crisis* (1973)
Rural District Councils Association. *Rural Transport: What Future Now?* (1971)
Welshpool & Llanfair RPS. *Cambrian Timetables 1904*
Wirral Railway Circle. *Cambrian Coast Express* (1973)

Working Timetables and Appendices, hold a wealth of information about closed lines and public timetables, original and reprints, complete the picture of operation. Major public libraries have collections of OS Maps, perhaps the most interesting being the 6-in editions around 1910. The new series of 1:50,000 maps that are replacing the standard 1-in series show many closed lines in much better detail, particularly so in the urban areas around Wrexham and Ruabon. Even better memory revivers of 'Dismantled Railways', as they are termed, are the new 1:25,000 (2½-in) maps. Grid references are standard.

Under 1974 local government reorganisation names of many districts have changed. I have retained the ones in use when the railways running through them were open.

Wrexham

Coppack, Tom. *A Lifetime with Ships*. Shipowner's racy stories about the past of Connah's Quay (1973)
Dow, George. *Great Central* (Vol 3—1965). (WM & CQ history)
Dunn, J. M. *Wrexham Mold & Connah's Quay Railway* (1957)
Hadfield, Charles. *Canals of the West Midlands* (David & Charles 1966)*
Lerry, G. G. *Collieries of Denbighshire* (second edition 1968)
Lerry, G. G. *Henry Robertson: Pioneer of Railways into Wales* (1949)
Lewin, H. G. *The Railway Mania and its Aftermath*
Reed, M. C. 'The Shrewsbury & Chester Railway', *Railway World* (October 1963)

Ryan, J. M. *Notes for Welsh Borders Brakevan Tour.* Wirral Railway Circle, 24 May 1969

Ruabon

Apart from the first three books, the Wrexham sources contain much useful information about the railways of Ruabon. *Canals of the West Midlands* is especially valuable.
Denton, J. H. *Railways & Waterways in North Wales*, Railway & Canal Historical Society, July 1969

Ruabon–Dolgelley; Bala–Blaenau Ffestiniog

Boyd, J. I. C. *Narrow Gauge Railways in South Caernarvonshire* (1973)*
Cockman, F. G. *Discovering Lost Railways* (1973)* Ffestiniog Rly. *Area Map and Track Diagram* (1969) clarifies position of its lines at Blaenau Ffestiniog
Lee, C. E. *Narrow Gauge Railways in North Wales* (1945)
Lloyd, M. 'Bala & Festiniog' (*Model Railway News*, May 1971)
Lloyd, M. E. M. 'Farewell to Bala–Blaenau Branch' (*Railway Magazine*, April 1961)
Stephenson Locomotive Society. *Souvenir of Last Passenger Train Bala–Blaenau Ffestiniog*, 22 January (1961)*

Cambrian Railways

Baddeley & Ward. *Through Guide to North Wales* (1904)
Bevan, G. P. *Tourists' Guide to the Wye* (1892)
Christiansen, Rex and Miller, R. W. *The Cambrian Railways* (Vol 1, Revised edition 1971 and Vol 2, 1968)*
Cozens, Lewis. Guides to the Kerry, Llanfyllin, Mawddwy and Van Railways
Gasquoine, C. P. *History of the Cambrian Railways* (1922)
Stephenson Locomotive Society. *Souvenir: Last Passenger Train Moat Lane–Brecon*, 30 December 1962. *Farewell to the Welshpool –Whitchurch and Ruabon–Barmouth lines*, 17 January 1965.

Jones E. V. *Mishaps on the Cambrian Railways* (1864–1922)

Kilvert, Rev Francis. *Kilvert's Diary* (edited: William Plomer)

Tolson, J. M. 'The Wrexham & Ellesmere Railway' (*Railway World*, June and July 1965)

Wren, W. J. *The Tanat Valley: Its Railways and Industrial Archaeology* (D. & C. 1969)*

Snowdonia

Bradley, V. J. *The Llanberis Lake Railway*, Industrial Railway Record (April 1972)

Clinker, C. R. *LNWR Chronology 1900–1960*

Dunn, J. M. *The Chester & Holyhead Railway* (Revised edition 1968)

Dunn, J. M. 'The Afon Wen Line', *Railway Magazine* (October 1958)

Dunn, J. M. 'The Anglesey Central Railway', *Railway Magazine* (April 1960)

Dunn, J. M. 'Penrhyn and Bethesda branches', *Railway Magazine* (October 1961)

Lee, C. E. *Narrow Gauge Railways in North Wales*

Lee, C. E. *The Penrhyn Railway* (1972)

Stones, H. R. 'Caernarvon Investiture 1911', *Railway Magazine* (July 1970)

Caernarvon County Council. *Objection to proposals to withdraw passenger services between Bangor and Afon Wen* (March 1964). Also: *Statements of Witnesses*

LNWR: North East Wales

Baughan, P. E. *The Chester & Holyhead Railway*, Vol 1 (1972)

Dean, R. J. *Historical Notes for a tour of Flintshire Railways*, Railway & Canal Historical Society (15 June 1968)

Dean, R. J. 'Ruthin & Cerrig-y-Druidion Railway', *Journal of the R & CHS* (October 1972)

Dean, R. J. 'The Vale of Clwyd Railway', *Journal of the R &
CHS* (July 1974)

Dunn, J. M. 'Vale of Clwyd Railway', *Railway Magazine*
(February 1957)

Dunn, J. M. 'Denbigh Ruthin & Corwen Railway', *Railway
Magazine* (March 1957)

Dunn, J. M. 'The Mold Railway', *Railway Magazine* (June
1962)

Dunn, J. M. 'The Mold & Denbigh Junction Railway', *Railway
Magazine* (July 1962)

Flintshire County Council. *Official Handbook* (*c*. 1945)

Mold. *Official Guide* (1937)

Acknowledgements

This volume has revived many boyhood memories and made writing an extra pleasure. Where my memory has erred, or sources have conflicted, I have been put back on the rails by my friend and co-author of the Cambrian and North Staffordshire Railway histories, Mr R. W. (Bob) Miller. Besides his meticulous checking of the manuscript, he has kept open a weather eye on the ever-changing scene on forgotten lines during his many journeyings into Wales. Mr Harold Forster, now BR Area Manager, Manchester, Piccadilly, and formerly Area Manager at Wrexham, and his successor, Mr Gordon Price, took me to the farthest parts of their territory.

I have drawn heavily on extended notes kindly provided by Messrs C. B. Pyne, County Planning Officer, Caernarvon; E. V. Jones, owner of the Severn Press at Newtown and author of *Mishaps on the Cambrian Railways 1864–1922*; and Stan Hugill, Bo'sun and Curator of the Outward Bound Maritime Museum at Aberdovey.

Other officials to whom I am indebted, whose posts may have changed under local government reorganisation, include Messrs C. A. J. Jacobs, now County Planning Officer, Clwyd; E. R. Luke, County Librarian and Archivist, Denbigh; A. G. Veysey, now County Archivist, Clwyd; G. Haulfryn Williams, County Archivist, Merioneth; G. Rhys Edwards, Information Officer, Snowdonia National Park.

Whitefield, Manchester   REX CHRISTIANSEN
1975

Index

INDEX

Severn Valley, 62, 65–6, 76, 78–9, 81
Shotton, 12, 14, 31–2
Shrewsbury, 19, 21–2, 75, 113
Snowdonia, 88–102
South Wales, 78–80
STATIONS:
 Arenig, 58
 Bala, *54*
 Bala Junction, 51, 52, 61, *54*
 Barmouth Junction, 50, 59, 61
 Berwyn, *36*
 Blaenau Ffestiniog, *71*
 Blodwell Junction, *89*
 Bodfari, *144*
 Buckley Junction, 12
 Builth Road, 78, 80, *107*
 Carrog, 53
 Cemmes Road, 82
 Coed Talon, *143*
 Corwen, *36*
 Dinas, *125*
 Dolgellau, *53*, *107*
 Holywell Town, *126*
 Llanfyllin, 72
 Llangollen, 55–6, *17*
 Llong, 114
 Maentwrog Road, *71*
 Moat Lane, 78, *90*
 Nantlle, *125*
 Oswestry, *72*
 Pantydwr, *90*
 Penmaenpool, 85–7
 Penyffordd, 104–5
 Penygroes, *108*
 Red Wharf Bay, *126*
 Shotton, 32
 Talyllyn, 78
 Three Cocks Junction, 78
 Wrexham Central, 24, 69, *18*
 Wrexham General, 24, 112
Stephenson, G., 21, 66, 88

Swindon, 63, 77

Talsarnau, 59
TRAIN SERVICES, *freight*:
 coal, 26, 111
 GWR pick-up, 113
 GCR, 69
 nuclear waste, 59
 ore, 20
 quarry, 73–5
 passenger:
 Land Cruises, 51, 101, 114, 116
 LNWR, 70, 100, 101, 110, 114–15
 Minera, 24
 Mold, 27
 Rhos, 41
 Ruabon, 45
Troop trains, 58
TRAMWAYS:
 Buckley, 122
 Henddu Dhu, 83
 Holywell, 110
 Kerry, 77
 Ruabon Brook, 39
Trams, electric, 41
Trawsfynydd, 11, 57–60, *54*
Trevor, 12, 41, 45, 48
Tryweryn reservoir, 57, 60–1

Vron branch: GWR, 20, 23–4;
Vyrnwy, Lake, 60, 74

Welshampton, 67
Welshpool, 62, 65, 70, 75
Whitchurch, 21, 46, 62, 64
Whittington, 66
Whixall Moss, 65–6
WM & CQ, 20, 23–4
Wrexham area, 12, 13, 20–33, 37, 39–47, 103–4, 112, 113, *17–18*, *35*
Wye Valley, 77